THE EVOLVING UNDERGRADUATE MAJOR

American Academy
of Physical Education Papers
No. 23

THE EVOLVING UNDERGRADUATE MAJOR

American Academy of Physical Education Papers No. 23

Sixty-First Annual Meeting
Boston, Massachusetts
April 18–19, 1989

Published by Human Kinetics Publishers
for the American Academy of Physical Education

Editors
Charles B. Corbin
Helen M. Eckert

Academy Seal designed by
R. Tait McKenzie

Managing Editor: Kathy Kane
Typesetter: Yvonne Winsor

ISBN 0-87322-278-4
ISSN 0741-4633
Copyright © 1990 by the American Academy of Physical Education

Library of Congress Cataloging-in-Publication Data

American Academy of Physical Education. Meeting (61st : 1989 :
    Boston, Mass.)
    The evolving undergraduate major : Sixty-first Annual Meeting,
    Boston, Massachusetts, April 18-19, 1989 / [editors, Charles B.
    Corbin, Helen M. Eckert].
        p. cm. -- (American Academy of Physical Education papers,
    ISSN 0741-4633 ; no. 23)
    Includes bibliographical references.
    ISBN 0-87322-278-4
    1. Physical education teachers--Training of--United States-
    -Congresses. I. Title. II. Series: American Academy of Physical
    Education. Meeting. Academy papers ; no. 23.
GV365.A47   1989   ∠8883
613.706'073--dc20   89-38751
                                                                 CIP

Printed in the United States of America
3 2 1

Human Kinetics Books
A Division of Human Kinetics Publishers, Inc.
Box 5076, Champaign, IL 61820
1-800-DIAL-HKP
1-800-334-3665 (in Illinois)

CONTENTS

The Evolving Undergraduate Major

Charles B. Corbin
Arizona State University

As the American Academy of Physical Education meets for this 61st time, we are considering the evolution of the undergraduate major. There is little question that much has changed since Luther Halsey Gulick declared physical education to be a "new profession" in 1890. His comments were made only 1 year after the Boston Conference in the Interest of Physical Training in 1889, an event in history that Park (1989) considers the beginning of physical education's first 100 years.

As the "new profession" of physical education begins its second 100 years, the Academy meets to debate its future. Has physical education evolved for the better since these early years? Will its evolution be planned and well thought out in the next 100 years?

Today I will concentrate my comments on the recent evolution of physical education as an undergraduate major. My assignment is to set the stage for the discussions that follow. Those interested in the early evolution of the "new profession" are referred to Park's excellent paper "The Second 100 Years" (Park, 1989).

Much of what we are here to discuss has its origins in the 1960s. It was during this time that dramatic shifts in the profession began to occur; its evolution accelerated. During this time "it is generally conceded that . . . something akin to a partial paradigmatic shift was occurring in physical education" (Park, 1989, p. 13). The American Academy of Physical Education and the Big Ten directors had made statements about the body of knowledge signaling a shift from the professional to the disciplinary in physical education. Franklin Henry's (1964) paper, "Physical Education—An Academic Discipline," has been considered a landmark in the evolution of physical education characterizing the shift. It could be said that the 1960s were the decade of change. This being the case, the 1950s can be characterized as the professional years. Most undergraduate programs in physical education were designed to prepare teachers and coaches for careers in public schools. In the 1960s this began to change (see Table 1).

The rapid evolution of undergraduate education in the 1960s occurred because major changes were taking place in all of higher education. However, the changes occurring at a few institutions did not necessarily reflect changes at the grass roots level. Thus, it was not until the 1970s that the full impact of the evolution of the 60s affected students in most undergraduate physical education programs. In the 1970s the focus of undergraduate physical education narrowed

Table 1

Changing Focus of Physical Education by Decades

Decade	Characterization	Focus
1950s	The professional years	Teaching Coaching
1960s	A time of change	Defining the discipline Planting seeds of change
1970s	Narrowing the focus	Emerging specialties Defining focus
1980s	Seeking identity	Are we a discipline? Are we a profession?

considerably. Those who taught in undergraduate programs became specialists or subspecialists, often in disciplinary areas rather than professional areas. Further, the areas of study commonly allied with physical education began to seek their own identities. Health, recreation, dance, and coaching, often areas of required study for all physical education majors, were deleted from undergraduate programs in physical education. Each became a separate area of study at most institutions. Credits previously devoted to study in these areas were often shifted to the study of the body of knowledge defined in the 1960s.

In the decade of the 1980s we have sought to find our identity. Park (1989) notes that "it may be useful to remember that medicine, an ancient and honored profession that many contend is the most valuable and venerated of the 20th century, was in a general state of disarray at the end of the 19th century . . . perhaps the new physical education is only now beginning to emerge?" (p. 20).

But what is physical education? Is it a discipline? Should the undergraduate program be a study of this discipline or body of knowledge? What is this body of knowledge? Does it change? Has it changed since it was defined in the 1960s? Is physical education a profession or series of professions? Clearly physical education evolved from a profession centered around school teaching. As Figure 1 illustrates, the profession of physical education centers around programs. Professionals deliver services to learners and clients by selecting appropriate programs and methodologies for meeting their unique needs. Professionals use evaluation techniques to determine if client–learner needs have been met.

The discipline is the body of knowledge that professionals use as the basis for their expertise. Should physical education focus on this expertise or on professional matters? Ellis (1987) suggests that both disciplinary and professional study are important, but that we should be careful not to overemphasize the discipline at the expense of the profession. Is there more than one physical education profession? And, if so, is the body of knowledge common to these professions? If we must prepare undergraduate students for both the discipline and the professions, what do we emphasize? These are all questions we are here today to try to answer.

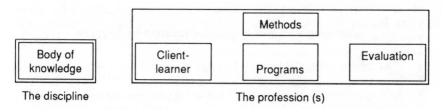

Figure 1 — Areas of undergraduate study: the discipline and the profession.

As I view other fields of study in the university, I note that some of the "hard" sciences appear to be disciplines looking for professions. Students preparing in disciplinary areas are looking for jobs. This is another characteristic of the 1980s, preparing for life's work. On the other hand, over the years, physical education might be characterized as a profession looking for a discipline. But is the discipline we have defined really the basis for our collective professions? Have be become too concerned with the discipline at the expense of the professions? The sessions at this 61st conference of the Academy are designed to answer questions such as this.

First, we will address the topic of the common body of knowledge. Clearly we have evolved since the first 100 years began in 1889. But has the discipline changed since it was more clearly defined in the 1960s? Is that discipline the core body of knowledge for our professions or merely a body of knowledge for a discipline? Does the body of knowledge need to be redefined? Is there a common core that all students in the collective fields of physical education must study? If yes, what is that common knowledge core?

Second, we will address teacher preparation. Is the common core of the discipline truly the basis for the study of the profession of physical education teaching? Should prospective teachers first study this core information and then study the profession of teaching? Can this be done in 4 years? Should we follow the recommendations of the Holmes Group?

Third, we will discuss undergraduate preparation in other physical education professions. Is the core of knowledge the basis for the education of sport managers, fitness leaders, exercise therapists, and other professions? Can these professionals be prepared in 4 years? or does it take 5? Should they be prepared in the discipline first with professional study to follow? or should disciplinary and professional study be intertwined?

Finally, we will discuss a name for the undergraduate major. Is physical education a name that adequately describes the discipline and all of the professions in the field? If not, what name does adequately describe them? As one of our speakers will indicate, there are more than 100 names given to departments that prepare undergraduate students in physical education. Does this lack of uniformity cause us problems? Would another name help us unify? Would there be other benefits in identifying the undergraduate major with a different name?

During the next 2 days we will discuss each of the issues described above. Clearly, physical education and its undergraduate major have evolved considerably in the last 100 years. With the explosion of knowledge and dramatic changes in our culture, the role of physical education changed, especially in the last 40 years. But has this evolution been a result of planning or haphazard change? Can a group such as the Academy play a significant role in planned change for the future?

As leaders in the field of physical education, will we merely discuss these issues as an academic exercise? Or will we take the lead in charting the course for the future? Will we lead or will we follow? As we start the second 100 years, the Academy can be proactive rather than reactive. Park (1989) entitled her paper "The Second 100 Years: Or, Can Physical Education Become the Renaissance Field of the 21st Century?". Will we be a part of the Renaissance? Will it happen? Can we help make it happen? Only time will tell.

References

ELLIS, M.J. (1988). Warning: The pendulum has swung far enough. *Journal of Physical Education, Recreation and Dance,* **58**(3), 75-78.

HENRY, F.M. (1964). Physical education: An academic discipline. *Journal of Health, Physical Education and Recreation,* **35**(7), 32-33.

PARK, R.J. (1989). The second 100 years: Or, can physical education become the renaissance field of the 21st century? *Quest,* **41**(1), 2-27.

The Body of Knowledge: A Common Core

Jerry R. Thomas
Arizona State University

With a rising sense of elation, *tnemevom* came to life all at once . . . He took a deep breath, tensed his muscles, and executed a back somersault with a half twist. He assumed a new dignity almost immediately as he realized that he now had a new name (that was quite simple to pronounce) and it was MOVEMENT . . . he realized that there was more to him than push-ups and jogging, as truly important as these parts of him might be. He sensed that he had physiological aspects, anatomical aspects, historical aspects, philosophical aspects, psychological aspects, sociological aspects, and so many other aspects that he couldn't count them on the fingers of his two hands.

This was an important realization for MOVEMENT, but he didn't rush off blindly to proclaim his glory to the world. He had learned his lesson. This time he would spell his name correctly, and he would rest his case for recognition on a sound scientific base . . . But let's not debate the issue for long since the sun is already quite high in the sky. (p. 53)

The quote above is from a paper Earl Zeigler (Zeigler, 1968) gave at the AAHPER annual meeting in St. Louis 21 years ago. Four years before that, in 1964, and subsequently in 1965 and 1966, the Big Ten directors (Zeigler & McCristal, 1967) focused on "The Body of Knowledge in Physical Education" and covered the topics in Table 1. Five of the topics are consistent across those meetings—history/philosophy of sport, exercise physiology, motor learning/sport psychology, biomechanics, and sport sociology—and probably represent much of what would currently be considered the body of knowledge for the study of human movement. This past December (1988), participants at the Big Ten/American Academy of Physical Education Leadership Conference in Chicago focused on renaming the field as well as defining appropriate content. Indeed, one wonders if we have debated the issue too long (25 years) and if the sun has already set.

However, I am not a pessimist. I believe we do have a legitimate field of study (I use that term advisedly instead of the term discipline), and I think we basically agree (at least as defined by our writings and practices) on the content of that field. In this paper I hope to accomplish three objectives. First, I will present information that indicates basic agreement concerning what should be included for undergraduate students in a core for the knowledge base of human movement. Second, I suggest that, while agreement exists concerning the core,

Table 1

Comparison of the Content of the Body of Knowledge in Physical Education Conferences Held by the Big Ten Directors in 1964, 1965, and 1966

1964	1965	1966
History of PE & sport	Philosophic research in PE & sport	History, philosophy, & comparative PE & sport
Exercise physiology	Exercise physiology	Exercise physiology
Biomechanics of human movement	Biomechanics	Biomechanics
Motor learning	Psychology & motor learning	Motor learning & sport psychology
Sport & culture	Sport & culture	Sociology of sport & PE
Human growth & development		Administrative theory

little agreement may exist about the level of knowledge or level of analysis at which information in the core should be presented. Third, I suggest that forms of movement should be included in the core, and that, indeed, they are an issue closely related to the level of knowledge to be presented.

Has a Core for the Study of Human Movement Been Identified?

The basis for the core was spelled out over 25 years ago, as listed in Table 1. In a follow-up to his classic paper of 1964 on the academic discipline, Franklin Henry (1978) argues that the academic discipline must be cross-disciplinary and be organized horizontally (as well as vertically). He suggests that the knowledge base of the discipline should include exercise physiology, motor learning, motor development, kinesiology, and the roles of athletics, dance, and other physical activities in the culture. Table 2 contains a comparison from four papers published between 1979 and 1987 suggesting the areas that represent the field of study. Taken together, the data (1964-1966 Big Ten directors, Henry, Haag, Lawson & Morford, Zeigler, and Thomas) published over the past 25 years shows remarkable similarity in defining the study of human movement.

This general approach can be related to architectonic attempts to categorize knowledge (e.g., Phenix, 1967) and is often used by universities to structure core experiences.[1] For example, movement would be classed under "types of skills"

---

[1]My thanks for this suggestion to Gary Krahenbuhl, Associate Dean, College of Liberal Arts and Sciences, Arizona State University.

Table 2

Comparisons of Areas Included in the Field of Study

Haag (1979)	Lawson & Morford (1979)	Zeigler (1983)	Thomas (1987)

Anatomical–physiological & motor function
  Sport medicine
  Sport biomechanics
	Biomechanics & biodynamics	Functional efficiency of physical activity
		
		Mechanical & muscular analysis of motor skills
			Physical foundations
			  Sport biomechanics
			  Sport physiology

Social & behavioral foundations
  Sport psychology
  Sport pedagogy
  Sport sociology
	Motor control	Motor learning & development	Social foundations
			  Sport psychology (motor learning & development)
			  Sport sociology

Historical–philosophical foundations
  Sport history
  Sport philosophy
	Sport studies	Sociocultural & behavioral aspects	Cultural foundations
			  Sport history
			  Sport philosophy
			  Sport pedagogy
			  Sport statistics

whereas knowledge about movement would be classed under "values and under-standings of knowledge."

Because there is considerable similarity between categories of knowledge about human movement, it seems reasonable to define this body of knowledge as the core for undergraduates who select human movement as a field of study. If pedagogy is considered to be the use of the body of knowledge to aid instruction, then the core can be defined as including the knowledge base (at an appropriate level of knowledge for undergraduates) from biomechanics; exercise physiology; history and philosophy of sport and physical activity; motor control, learning, and development; psychology of exercise and sport; and sport sociology. The officers in the Academy who plan the program appear to support these six categories as the core because they serve as the basis for organizing two recent publications: *The Academy Papers* of 1982 (*Synthesizing and Transmitting Knowledge: Research and Its Application*) and 1986 (*The Cutting Edge in Physical Education and Exercise Science Research*). These areas include the concepts of:

- human anatomy/function,
- physical growth and motor development,
- biomechanical aspects of movement,
- acute and chronic effects of exercise,
- behavioral and neuromuscular control of movement,
- motor skill acquisition,
- psychological factors in movement, exercise, and sport,
- sociocultural factors in movement, exercise, and sport, and
- history/philosophy of movement, exercise, and sport.

With appropriate prerequisites from the traditional disciplines in the physical, biological, and social sciences (Henry, 1978), a curriculum can be planned to systematically present the nine concepts listed as aspects of knowledge about human movement. However, one should note, as Hanna (1961) does, "Any attempt at structuring knowledge is at best an approximation and must be recognized for what it is—the product of a human brain creating some system for organizing the vast quantities of sense data that flow in constantly through the receptors of the nervous system" (p. 70). However, "For the most efficient learning to occur, it would appear that units of instruction should be formed according to the structural patterns of the discipline" (Phenix, 1967, p. 35). Thus, it seems appropriate to include the concepts listed in such courses as exercise physiology, biomechanics, and sport psychology. Yet the question remains, how many courses are required to cover the appropriate content? Is the amount of knowledge necessary in the core greater in exercise physiology than in sport sociology? This question involves not only the quantity of knowledge that is essential to the core, but the level at which that knowledge is to be presented.

One final point—I have suggested only one way in which knowledge about human movement may be organized—the rather traditional structure around subareas of specialization. Other options exist. For example, in writing about medical education, Nabel (1985) suggested that knowledge from biology could be ordered in the following manner: molecular basis of biologic evolution; cellular organization; generation of organ systems; the human as individual; and human-kind, environment, and social development. Knowledge about human movement could also be ordered from a levels-of-analysis perspective. However, levels of knowledge could also be viewed from a subarea perspective.

Are Levels of Knowledge an Issue?

While faculty who prepare undergraduates to study human movement might generally agree on the description of content by concepts and course title, considerable disagreement is likely on the level at which that content is to be presented. The level of knowledge (or level of analysis) presented may also influence the subsequent use of that knowledge in more professionally oriented programs (e.g., teaching, medicine, fitness education). As an example, information from exercise physiology might be presented at the conceptual level with the intent that the concepts serve as the basis for later work in fitness education. Or, knowledge might be presented at a systems level where the acute and chronic effects of exercise are evaluated as they influence the cardiovascular and muscular systems. Or, knowledge about cellular response to exercise might be presented. Each of these approaches suggests very different classroom and laboratory experiences for the undergraduate student in exercise physiology. The approaches also suggest very different intents for use of the knowledge in professional settings.

I suggest, as have others (e.g., Singer, 1979), that faculties at different institutions, even major research institutions, may view the level of knowledge to be presented in very different ways. Can a core body of knowledge be defined apart from the level at which the information will be presented? This issue is related to a second point. "While physical activity is consistently identified as the focus of the field, *which* physical activity is central has not been agreed upon" (Rose, 1986, p. 11). Generally, we have shown more interest in overhand striking patterns in tennis players than in carpenters, locomotion in humans than in cats, mental practice in high jumpers than in metal riveters. If we define the study of human movement in generic terms, as opposed to using such delimiters as exercise, sport, games, and play, do we teach the undergraduate core at a different level? Do university departments use varying delimiters to reflect the levels of knowledge they teach to undergraduates who major in the study of human movement? If yes, what is represented by a degree in human movement? If no, what level of knowledge is appropriate for undergraduates? Is it possible or reasonable to approach every course from a levels-of-knowledge perspective? If it is, do we have faculty who can do that effectively? These questions are not asked only by me, nor are they necessarily recent (e.g., Singer, 1979).

Should Movement Performance be Part of the Core?

A second difficult issue is, What is the place of human movement performance in the study of movement? One way of knowing is through the experience of performance. This emphasis on performance separates dance as well as athletics from our field of study. There have always been voices calling for more emphasis on movement performance in the body of knowledge. Brown stressed this issue in her paper in *Quest* in the 1967 issue focusing on the discipline of human movement. Broekhoff (1979) and Seidentop (1980) have both pointed out that the instructional content for our field is the movements themselves. Most recently,

Kleinman (1988) has renewed this call, suggesting that the athlete performing is a legitimate field of study just as is the dancer dancing. What is, or should be, the relationship between physical activity and the study of it? Part of our problem can be explained if we understand that human movement and the study of human movement fall under different generic classes of knowledge (Phenix, 1967). Human movement is classed as "singular form" (the realm of aesthetic meanings), whereas the study of human movement is classed as "general fact" (general forms that become related to actuality—empirics). That is, the study of human movement focuses on the description, explanation, and prediction of regularities.

Many of the members of the Academy came into this field as a result of sport and athletic performance. Can we afford to prepare undergraduates in the study of human movement who cannot themselves move efficiently and effectively? If your answer is no, then what forms of movement must they master? If your answer is yes, I am terrified of the implications. What will happen to a field of study in which the scholars have not mastered and do not understand through experience the essential nature of the field—movement? I am not even going to address a possible yes answer.

If you said that people who prepare themselves with an undergraduate degree in human movement should themselves move with skill, then what skills should they possess and to what degree? Does a paraplegic who can skillfully control a wheelchair qualify? does a skilled carpenter? a skilled athlete? Is skillful performance in one area sufficient? Or is a moderate quality of the performance required in several areas? Is the quality of the performance even the issue? Is the process of experiencing various movement forms the point?

A related but important question is, Are movement forms an essential part of what is to be learned? If so, how much a part? Should the degree be a performance one? Or should performance skills already be present in the person who wants to study movement? Essentially this is a question of whether movement skill is a prerequisite to the scientific study of movement.

What Does All This Mean?

I believe if we are to have a legitimate field of study, we must have a core that everyone who seeks an undergraduate major in that field completes. I also believe we are in basic agreement about what constitutes that core (and have been for 25 years). If this is true, and the Academy were to agree in principle, then universities and colleges must be consistent in including the core body of knowledge in students' programs. We cannot offer degrees in the study of human movement that allow omission of important topics in human movement, regardless of the ultimate intent of the user. In this regard we cannot be user-friendly.

Much more difficult issues—and issues that do relate to the ultimate intent of the user—are the level of knowledge that is presented and the degree and nature of movement skill required. I have recommendations on both issues. Using exercise physiology as an example, I suggest we present material to undergraduates at the systems level but bring the other two levels into instruction. That is, cellular functions can frequently be used as explanations for system responses and concepts related to humans exercising can be used as examples for application of system functions. This approach offers a focus for everyone, at the same time acknowledging the need for understanding different levels. Some (e.g., Martens, 1987) have suggested that movement, sport, and exercise cannot be studied usefully except within environmental contexts. Does that concept have important implications for the level at which knowledge is presented?

I also believe skills in movement forms should be required in the core. I readily admit that this belief is much more intuitive than other points I have made in this paper. This comes from my own research focus in studying the relation of the sport knowledge base and sport performance. Simply stated, one who has no expertise in a sport cannot study the skilled nature of the behavior satisfactorily. This statement is based on experience which, admittedly, is not the highest form of scientific knowledge. However, experience should not be regarded lightly. I recommend that undergraduate students who seek a degree in the study of human movement should be required to show competence in several movement forms (e.g., sports, dance). However, I choose to leave the exact nature of the movement forms to be required to another time, place, and person.

A rather interesting final question is, Should a student majoring in human movement also be expected to show some degree of health-related physical fitness? Because much of exercise physiology relates to this question, and because much of skillful performance is based on minimal levels of cardiovascular and muscular fitness, as well as flexibility, I believe it is a reasonable expectation that people who study movement should have and maintain an acceptable level of health-related physical fitness.

References

ACADEMY Papers, The. Synthesizing and transmitting knowledge: Research and its applications. (1982). Reston, VA: AAHPERD.

ACADEMY Papers, The. The cutting edge in physical education and exercise science research. (1986). Champaign, IL: Human Kinetics.

BROEKHOFF, J. (1979). Physical education as a profession. *Quest*, **31**, 244-254.

BROWN, C. (1967). The structure of knowledge of physical education. *Quest*, **9**(Winter), 53-67.

HAAG, H. (1979). Development and structure of a theoretical framework for sport science. *Quest*, **31**, 25-35.

HANNA, P.R. (1961). Structure of knowledge: The interrelationship of ideas. In W.A. Jenkins (Ed.), *The nature of knowledge: Implications for the education of teachers* (pp. 68-82). Milwaukee: E.A. Uhrig Foundation.

HENRY, F.M. (1978). The academic discipline of physical education. *Quest*, **29**, 13-29.

KLEINMAN, S. (1988, December). *Performance, participation and study of physical activity.* Paper presented at the Big Ten/AAPE Conference, Chicago.

LAWSON, H.A., & Morford, W.R. (1979). The crossdisciplinary structure of kinesiology and sports studies: Distinctions, implications, and advantages. *Quest*, **31**, 222-230.

MARTENS, R. (1987). Science, knowledge, and sport psychology. *The Sport Psychologist*, **1**, 29-55.

NABEL, G.J. (1985). Order and human biology. *The American Journal of Medicine,* **78,** 545-548.

PHENIX, P.H. (1967). The architectonics of knowledge. *Quest,* **9**(Winter), 28-41.

ROSE, D.A. (1986). Is there a discipline of physical education? *Quest,* **38,** 1-21.

SEIDENTOP, D. (1980). *Physical education: Introductory analysis.* Dubuque, IA: Wm. C. Brown.

SINGER, R.N. (1979). Future directions in the movement arts and sciences. *Quest,* **31,** 255-263.

THOMAS, J.R. (1987). Are we already in pieces, or just falling apart? *Quest,* **39,** 114-121.

ZEIGLER, E.F. (1968). A tale of two titles. *Journal of Health, Physical Education and Recreation,* **39**(5), 53.

ZEIGLER, E.F. (1983). Relating a proposed taxonomy of sport and developmental physical activity to a planned inventory of scientific findings. *Quest,* **35,** 54-65.

ZEIGLER, E.F., & McCristal, K.J. (1967). A history of the Big Ten Body-of-Knowledge Project in physical education. *Quest,* **9**(Winter), 79-84.

Reactions to "The Body of Knowledge: A Common Core"

Michael J. Ellis
University of Oregon

In my scheme of things the needs of the professions drive the nature and content of scholarly activity in the field. The field and its attendant disciplines exist because of a compact struck between our society and members of the field. Resources are directed to us with the expectation that we will alter the likelihood that people will live higher quality lives and that the nation's stock of human capital will be improved. Our support will depend directly on the extent to which we can reliably produce desired effects. We are, as are all professions, charged with the responsibility for engineering effects, not simply knowing. The current and future needs of the professions should thus dictate the kinds of questions asked by the researchers associated with the field. Further, the basic core of knowledges to be communicated to all professional practitioners should derive its coherence from the projected needs of the professional.

Having established the primacy of the profession, at least for the purpose of my reaction, let it be made quite clear that this does not preclude the conduct of scholarship of the highest quality. It is just that the researchers and scholars should be forever mindful that their work is only justified by the potential understanding the fundamental processes of human movement brings to the practice of countless professionals. The building of the body of theory should address human movement and be informed by its potential for possible use. The targetless efforts to simply understand phenomena may, and I say may, be supported in the colleges of arts and sciences without expectation of use. (However, in my university I note increasing attention is given to those areas in the arts and sciences that are believed to be potentially valuable, e.g., optics, theater, artificial intelligence, materials science, etc.). Those who wish to explore phenomena in isolation of any responsibility for benefiting the professions are best located in the cognate disciplines in the colleges of arts and sciences. We have such scarce resources in our own departments that we cannot afford to support people who would be more comfortable without some responsibility for underpinning the professions.

The various professions structuring human movement to influence the quality of human life derive their power by developing reliable technologies from the theories of the fundamental processes. Thus, the body of human movement science and professional practice are interlinked. The output from one forms the input to the other. This relationship is reflected in the papers presented in this volume by Thomas and Newell. Both argue that because all human movement professions are based in the arts and sciences of human movement, then the core concepts form the basis upon which all the professions rest. It is this core of knowledge that links all practice to the human movement itself and it is thus necessary for all professionals in the field. A common integrated body of experience, vocabulary, and theory becomes even more critical when the rapidity with which the various professional outlets have diverged is considered. A counter to the centrifugal influences of specialization is necessary. Finally, the likelihood that professional outlets will change during the course of a career also argues that fundamental principles become the bedrock of the field, not the narrow and changing technologies.

Newell refers to the body of knowledge that can be symbolized and that results from systematic enquiry into the fundamental processes of human movement as "declarative knowledge." This knowledge domain incorporates the body of theory and informs, and is informed by (according to his schema), the action knowledge that results from humans moving and the technical knowledge that supports the professions.

The fundamental body of declarative knowledge needed by all human movement professionals has come during the last 25 years to be structured along the lines of the specialties, which in turn are organized along the traditional structure of the cognate disciplines. Thomas' paper reflects that, and I would like to elaborate his structure to present an inclusive taxonomy of the body of knowledge about human movement studies (see Figure 1). This schema simply arranges the traditional structure of academic organization into a hierarchy according to the scale of the phenomena considered at each level. It suggests the traditional structure of the research specialties. The course work, staffing patterns, and research specialties in the field have simply and conveniently mirrored this taxonomy.

The simplification of structuring the field along the lines of the taxonomy brings two major shortcomings. First, there is a real danger that, as the status of human movement studies and the professions that it informs rises, these studies are more likely to be co-opted by the cognate disciplines desperate to find avenues to utility. This has been called "agenda piracy" by Lawson. As our courses, labs, specializations, and specialists are identified by names and content that ape the cognate disciplines rather than declaring the human movement phenomena they are trying to understand, then the greater is this threat. The second disadvantage stems from the fragmentation of knowledge and the difficulty that students have in integrating that knowledge into useful theory structures that bear some connection to the whole human movement complex context.

The solution to this double difficulty is beginning to emerge. The debates in the leadership conferences in Chicago and Boston have suggested that knowledge domains should be assembled around clusters of coherent concepts that derive their nature from the phenomenon of human movement and not from the structure of the traditional academic disciplines. The first suggestions are the following:

- Energy, work, and efficiency;
- Coordination, control, and skill;
- Growth, development, and form;
- Involvement, enculturation, and achievement.

DOMAINS OF DECLARATIVE KNOWLEDGE

OF HUMAN MOVEMENT

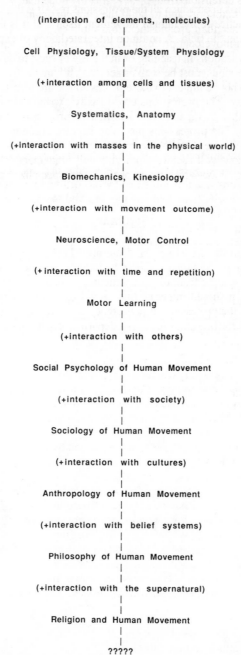

(interaction of elements, molecules)
|
Cell Physiology, Tissue/System Physiology
|
(+interaction among cells and tissues)
|
Systematics, Anatomy
|
(+interaction with masses in the physical world)
|
Biomechanics, Kinesiology
|
(+interaction with movement outcome)
|
Neuroscience, Motor Control
|
(+interaction with time and repetition)
|
Motor Learning
|
(+interaction with others)
|
Social Psychology of Human Movement
|
(+interaction with society)
|
Sociology of Human Movement
|
(+interaction with cultures)
|
Anthropology of Human Movement
|
(+interaction with belief systems)
|
Philosophy of Human Movement
|
(+interaction with the supernatural)
|
Religion and Human Movement
|
?????

Figure 1 — The domains of declarative knowledge of human movement.

While this may not be the final arrangement of the concepts, it presents an example of how to integrate declarative knowledge in integrated packages in a structure that is defensible from piracy. It is my hope that we are able to refine and develop this taxonomy and to build the core curriculum around the integrative concepts rather than around the subdisciplines.

The human movement professions referred to in this paper go beyond the traditional specializations in teaching or in the use of sport to develop the nation's youth. The professions must be seen as serving all humans from womb to tomb. They should also not be limited to those professions using structured sport, dance, exercise, and play. The professions could easily expand over the next 25 years to include the other therapeutic and habilitative processes of occupational and physical therapy. The professions may also capture ergonomics or human factors and form alignments with the health enhancement industry. These even broader conceptions will require a unifying and fundamental body of core curricula experiences upon which many professional specialized technologies may be built.

Summary

A core curriculum should deliver the declarative knowledge underpinning all the human movement professions. It should be integrated around a conceptual structure that derive its logic from the phenomena of human movement, not the cognate disciplines. It should integrate that knowledge in ways that illuminate the real problems of the professions it is designed to serve rather than reflecting the conveniences of staffing the university department with subspecialists.

Reactions to Thomas and Newell

Roberta J. Park
University of California, Berkeley

When we ask the question, What should be the core of an undergraduate degree program? we are asking what knowledge, understanding, and technical skills an individual should possess who claims to have been prepared in a particular field. Moreover, because technical skills are based on knowledge and understanding, we seem to be driven back to that much-debated question, Is there a discipline called physical education (or kinesiology or sport and exercise science)? And, if so, of what is it constituted?

Both Thomas and Newell believe there is such a discipline and that students should partake of something amounting to a common core. As Thomas has pointed out, the basis for such a core was spelled out 25 years ago. Drawing from several major reports, he observes that the following courses have been included in most proposals: biomechanics; exercise physiology; history and philosophy of sport and physical activity; motor control, learning, and development; psychology of exercise and sport; and sport sociology.

Approaching the topic in a slightly different manner, Newell has proposed four broadly defined subject-matter categories as the core experiences of an undergraduate degree in kinesiology: (a) energy, work, and efficiency; (b) coordination, control, and skill; (c) growth, development, and form; and (d) social practices and values. At this stage of the field's evolution, Newell's approach offers the advantage of sufficient flexibility to accommodate variously labeled and structured courses. His approach may help us to overcome some of our stubborn tendencies to give preferential treatment to courses with certain titles. The more conventionally named content areas set forth by Thomas can be easily subsumed within the four categories offered by Newell. However, designations like exercise physiology and sport psychology have lengthy and, in general, respected traditions, and they are easily recognizable to those outside our field. We should not forget that in the academic world, as elsewhere, words are powerful conveyers of meanings—both explicit and implicit.

I believe, as I think Jerry and Karl do, that considerably more agreement exists regarding something like a common core than we might believe, given the spate of recent (and generally fruitful) debates over specialization and fragmentation (e.g., Hoffman, 1985; Thomas, 1985; Greendorfer, 1987). A more difficult question is probably Thomas' second point, namely, the "level of knowledge or level of analyses at which information in the core should be presented." In various significant ways, this issue is related to Newell's observation that primary specializations must be related to and integrated with a student's broader intellectual development. Taken together, these two points constitute a major challenge for us all. Stated simply, this is, How can students achieve the needed depth in the constituent parts and at the same time acquire the desired breadth?

This question is currently being debated in a number of fields, especially in medicine and the biological sciences. It has also driven several major reports concerning American higher education. Departments of physical education (or kinesiology, or exercise and sport sciences), as have other fields, must come to an intelligent resolution if they are to survive. Fortunately, our field embraces the scope that other fields are now seeking to define for themselves.

Concerned that a shift away from traditional liberal education to vocational training was not adequately preparing students to deal with a complex and rapidly changing world, educators, legislators, scientists, and thoughtful Americans in the 1970s began to call for educational reforms. Not only were the public schools indicted, but also the training of teachers and collegiate education, in general. The Carnegie Foundation for the Advancement of Teaching labeled general education a disaster, and the U.S. Commissioner of Education "called for the creation of a core curriculum that would emphasize our common needs and thereby increase the chances of survival for the human species" (Gaff, 1983). Reviewing Allan Bloom's (1987) controversial best-seller on the failures of American education, *The Closing of the American Mind*, Sydney Hook (1989) offered his own proposals regarding what students need to know: (a) comprehension of different types of discourse and the ability to express oneself in a literate manner; (b) knowledge of one's body and mind, of the world of nature, and of the scientific method; (c) an understanding of how society functions and of the historical, social, and economic forces that have shaped our past and are likely to influence our future; (d) the ability to differentiate between arbitrary and reasonable judgments of value; and (e) an understanding of evidence, relevance, and the canons of validity.

If students are to achieve such knowledge, they must have teachers whose own education has prepared them in such a way that they can provide the needed learning experiences. Not surprisingly, therefore, the education of American teachers has been the topic of some of the most intense and sustained criticisms. Worried that the typical teacher-education curriculum (with its plethora of methodology as opposed to subject-matter courses) had enfeebled the teaching force, researchers called for reforms ranging from relatively minor modifications to major overhauls. Pointing out that the implementation of the 1910 Flexner Report "transformed medical practice in the United States by insisting on rigorous preparation of physicians" (p. 7), the Carnegie Forum on Education (1986) called for sweeping changes that give to subject matter a central and substantial place in the undergraduate curriculum. The Holmes Group (1986) recommended that the general educational background of teachers should be at least as substantial as that required of students in liberal arts and sciences and that clinical aspects of teacher preparation must be better integrated with subject-matter components (Razor, 1988).

At the same time, concerned that the explosion of knowledge and the need for specialization was producing professionals who were "unable to address themselves to significant issues underpinning their own activities" (Gaff, 1983, pp. 2, 25), thoughtful individuals in law, medicine, engineering, science, and other fields became alerted to the dangers of a too narrowly focused undergraduate curriculum.

Most current proposals for curricular reform, therefore, maintain that such specialization as is necessary must be balanced by experiences that stress the integration of knowledge. Institutions that had formerly emphasized extensive professional preparation curricula are once again "reaffirming the value of the liberal arts as the most generically useful knowledge produced by the human mind" (Gaff, 1983, p. 65) and insisting that specialized skills and professional training must be carefully related to a comprehensive core composed of arts and science courses.

Similar discussions have been occurring in medicine and the biological sciences where the explosion of knowledge has been especially intense. The Association of American Medical Colleges recently asserted that the undergraduate education of physicians "must encompass broad study in the humanities and in the social as well as the natural sciences" (Levy, 1988, p. 130). The lengthy report "Physicians for the 21st Century" (1984), concluded that medical students must have experiences with "essential knowledge in both basic and clinical sciences" (p. 122). Discussing "the new biology in relation to medical education," Daniel Tosteson (1983) proposed a 4-year curriculum in which all students would share the same learning experiences for about half of their studies and devote the other half to elective courses. As they progressed, increasing attention was to be devoted to the clincial arts and sciences. Such a program, Tosteson maintains, "would graduate a physician qualified to enter training in any specialty" (pp. 20-21). Having reviewed the intellectual and social structure of science in the United States since the 1960s, David Remington (1988) declared that some fields appear to be in danger of becoming "increasingly isolated from the synergistic cross-fertilization of ideas, techniques and conceptual tools coming from other fields" (p. 63). Such "baroque" fields, he maintains, risk losing their vitality. These points seem especially pertinent to the theme of these 1989 American Academy of Physical Education meetings.

In the Western world, the initiation of formal interest in physical education is usually located in Classical Greece. By the time of Plato and Aristotle (ca. 427-322 B.C.), well-articulated theories of *physis* (body) and *psyche* (soul/mind) related physical education to both therapeutics or medicine and to the proper and full development of the individual citizen. Shortly after the founding of the American Association for Physical Education, Luther Halsey Gulick (1890) declared physical education to be a profession grounded in anatomy, physiology, psychology, history, and philosophy. Three years later Thomas Dennison Wood (1894) stated: "There is today, in embryonic and crude form, a science of physical education which offers work for the biologist, and physiologist, the psychologist, and the general educator" (p. 621). These and numerous other major statements and events during the last 100 years give support to the contention that physical education is quintessentially a *biopsychosocial* field. (The term *biocultural* would possibly be a better choice, but as yet most individuals outside of anthropology still define "culture" too narrowly and superficially.)

If we would remind ourselves that throughout history the most powerful and influential statements regarding physical education have typically characterized it as biopsychosocial—and having important links to health and human development—we might be able to avoid much of the now stale debate regarding what types of subject matter an undergraduate major should include. Moreover, if we would also remind ourselves that theory and practice are always linked, and that significant questions may be generated (or answered) in either domain, we might reduce the amount of time and energy that has been consumed in arguments over which is the more essential. Depending upon desired outcomes, somewhat more weight may be placed upon one or the other; but, in any circumstance, it is quality far more than quantity that is important.

Recently, two useful models have appeared in the literature that might help our thinking about these matters. In "The Biopsychosocial Model and Medical Education: Who Are to Be the Teachers?" George Engel (1982) maintains that the medical profession has unwittingly created and sustained artificial dichotomies by divorcing biomedical from psychosocial studies. He proposes a model for medical education that is based upon a "hierarchy of natural systems" to replace the standard medical curriculum. This would include studies ranging from subatomic particles to the biosphere with the individual human being placed at the highest level of the organ/nervous system hierarchy and at the lowest level of the social systems hierarchy. In a similar manner, Gary Nabel (1985) has proposed a model for an integrated medical education that embraces molecular, cellular, organ system, individual, and social/historical/cultural studies.

The above-mentioned models suggest a curricular arrangement that is not very different from the undergraduate programs that have been proposed in numerous influential statements since the early 1960s. These statements hold that our students need to know about structure and function and how they relate to human performance from infancy through old age for the highly skilled, the average citizen, and those who have various limiting conditions. Students need to understand the role of physical activity in the maintenance of health and fitness and about central nervous system processing and how this is related to a range of human movement skills. They need to know how the human organism develops biologically, psychologically, and socially, and they need to know something about the role of play, games, sports, and exercise and physical activity in human cultures (both contemporary and historical). Whether these competencies are gained under the rubric of traditional titles such as sport psychology, exercise physiology, motor control, and history of sport and physical education or in area studies like energy, work, and efficiency; coordination, control, and skill; growth, development, and form; and social and cultural practices and values does not seem especially compelling. What is important is that they are gained!

Just how such experiences are to be arranged in the curriculum and how much weight will be given to each will depend upon the missions, organizational structures, and goals of each institution and where its physical education unit is located (own school, liberal arts college, college of education). The quality of the experiences will be strongly influenced by the training of those faculty members who teach in the undergraduate curriculum. It is here that we presently face some of our most critical challenges. Faculty whose own undergraduate (and graduate) education was characterized by a dearth of subject-matter courses will not be well prepared for the physical education of the 1990s unless they have taken the initiative to adapt to the new forces shaping the field. These individuals will need encouragement to retool or in other ways contribute the knowledge they have gained from years of dedicated service. At the same time they must be convinced that many curricula will have to change and it cannot be "business as usual."

The question of whether performance should be part of an undergraduate major and, if so, what part, has been addressed by both Newell and Thomas. Its answer depends largely upon desired outcomes. If one is planning a career in teaching, or exercise prescription, or any number of areas in which performance is a major component, the curriculum must provide ample room for appropriate amounts and quality. We are likely, I think, to find fairly broad agreement here. It is less likely, however, that there will be anywhere near as much agreement on the question, Should performance be an essential element for *all* majors? Yet skilled performance in the motor domain certainly seems logical, legitimate, and desirable. In our haste to reject the much-maligned older programs that were filled with skill development courses, we must be cautious that we do not let academic snobbery force us into a senseless posture.

Colleges and universities typically include a cluster of disciplines labeled performing arts (e.g., music, art, drama). No one seems troubled that they require students to attain a specified level of performance skill. (However, we must recognize that one can study art history and not be required to take a single performance course.) Architecture students are required to construct models of buildings they have designed; an engineering curriculum is likely to include surveying and allied skills. Biomedical physics students will be expected to develop skills in the use of the electron microscope. Are these not performance skills? By their nature, some majors necessitate more hands-on clinical, applied, or performance abilities than do others. It is reasonable to expect physical education majors to attain a certain amount of performance skill as well. But to what extent—and how is this to be gained? Local circumstances will greatly influence decisions.

For 16 years I taught a course in applied biomechanics for prospective teachers that focused on a wide range of performance skills (e.g., tennis serve, drive in field hockey, walking on crutches, wrist wrestling, hammering, ladder climbing, etc.). Engineering students who enrolled in this course found it to be interesting and worthwhile, as did physical education majors. At some institutions, a limited number of carefully designed performance experiences developed around such a course might be an acceptable part of the undergraduate major curriculum. At other institutions, faculty senates and committees on courses may be likely to endorse substantially more.

I agree absolutely with Karl Newell that because missions vary from institution to institution, and because local circumstances will always impose limits and foster possibilities, we cannot expect any absolutely universal curriculum, although we might advocate a common core. Jerry Thomas has mentioned Franklin Henry's 1978 paper in which Henry's ideas regarding "the discipline" were most fully explicated. Let us remember that Henry never intended to suggest that all institutions should offer identical curricula. Each would be influenced by its unique circumstances. Although we should not seek to clone any particular program, it is likely that peer institutions will increasingly develop undergraduate majors that share a number of common characteristics. It is likely, also, that increasing attention will be directed to subject-matter courses as we move toward the 21st century.

References

BLOOM, A.D. (1987). *The closing of the American mind*. New York: Simon & Schuster.

CARNEGIE Forum on Education and the Economy. Task Force on Teaching as a Profession. (1986). *A nation prepared: Teachers for the 21st century*. New York: Carnegie Corporation.

ENGEL, G.L. (1982). The biopsychosocial model and medical education: Who are to be the teachers? *New England Journal of Medicine*, **306**(13), 802-805.

GAFF, J.G. (1983). *General education today: A critical analysis of controversies, practices, and reforms*. San Francisco: Jossey-Bass.

GREENDORFER, S.L. (1987). Specialization, fragmentation, integration, discipline, profession: What is the real issue? *Quest*, **39**(1), 56-64.

GULICK, L.H. (1890). Physical education: A new profession. *Proceedings of the 5th Annual Meeting of the American Association for the Advancement of Physical Education* (pp. 59-66). New York: Andrus & Church.

HENRY, F.M. (1978). The academic discipline of physical education. *Quest*, **29**, 13-29.

HOFFMAN, S.J. (1985, August). Specialization + fragmentation = extermination: A formula for the demise of graduate education. *Journal of Physical Education, Recreation and Dance*, **56**(6), 19-21.

HOLMES Group Report, The. Tomorrow's teachers: A report of the Holmes Group. (1986). East Lansing, MI: Holmes Group, Inc.

HOOK, S. (1989). The closing of the American mind: An intellectual best-seller revisited. *American Scholar*, **58**(1), 123-135.

LEVY, H.R. (1988). The impact of science on medicine. In P.T. Marsh (Ed.), *Contesting the boundaries of liberal and professional education: The Syracuse experiment* (pp. 130-139). New York: Syracuse University Press.

NABEL, G.J. (1985). Order and human biology. *American Journal of Medicine*, **78**, 545-548.

PHYSICIANS for the 21st century. (1984). *Journal of Medical Education*, **59**(11), Part 2.

RAZOR, J.E. (1988). The Holmes Group proposal and implications for physical education as a "solid" subject matter (and other related problems). *Quest*, **40**(1), 33-46.

REMINGTON, J.A. (1988). Beyond big science in America: The binding of inquiry. *Social studies of science: An international review of research in the social dimension of science and technology*, **18**(1), 45-72.

THOMAS, J.R. (1985). Are we already in pieces, or just falling apart? *Quest*, **39**(2), 114-121.

TOSTESON, D.C. (1983). Teaching the new biology [Keynote]. In C.P. Friedman and E.F. Purcell (Eds.), *The new biology and medical education: Merging the biological, information, and cognitive sciences*. New York: Josiah Macy, Jr. Foundation.

WOOD, T.D. (1894). Some unsolved problems in physical education. In NEA (Ed.), *Proceedings of the International Congress of Education of the World's Columbian Exposition* (pp. 621-623). New York: J.J. Little & Co.

The Extended Education Model: Part of the Solution

Michael G. Maksud
Oregon State University

A nation at risk! A rising tide of mediocrity! These were the headlines that stung the educational establishment and shocked, once again, the American public in 1983 with the publication of the National Commission on Excellence in Education report, *A Nation at Risk: The Imperative for Educational Reform*. The issue has not gone away. In May 1988 *Newsweek* published an article, "A Nation Still at Risk," noting some progress but suggesting that much more needs to be done.

The failures of American public education continue. In my view the failures are both relative and relevant. We are failing relative to our capacity to do better. The failures are relevant because they handicap our intellectual potential. Examples of the failures abound; they are documented in the professional literature as well as in the popular press. The dropout rates among our high school students are alarming—approaching 40% in some states (Hodgkinson, 1985). In Oregon approximately 25% of the students drop out of high school. In some economically depressed areas the numbers are much higher.

An estimated 13% of 17-year-olds are considered functional illiterates. Two thirds of the people in our correctional institutions are illiterate; about 80% of them are high-school dropouts (Perpich, 1989).

For those students who stay in school, serious questions have been raised regarding the quality of their education. Their understanding of history and current events is seriously lacking. Many students do not know when the Civil War occurred or what happened at Chernobyl. In a world of growing interdependence we fail to recognize the values of bilingualism. In an age of increasing technology too many of our students are mathematical morons. In a recent six-nation study, conducted by the Educational Testing Service, eighth graders in the U.S. ranked last—dead last (Halpert, 1989). We were also near the bottom in science. In an information age we continue to apply concepts that were appropriate to an agricultural society; we must prepare students beyond personal hygiene and home economics.

The failures of American public education are shared. It is inappropriate to lay the blame entirely on our public schools and universities. Sharing in the failure is the American family, our political institutions, and society in general. The background, the climate, the very foundation of an effective education originates in the home. In my view that foundation is weak. It is weakened by

23

ever increasing divorce rates and single-parent families, by dual career/working parents, by increasing competition for the child's time and energy (including television), in some cases by abusive parents, and all too often by lack of basics such as food and housing.

Our political institutions are failing to meet their responsibility to public education. Legislators nationally do not view public education as a national priority, essential to the economic vitality of our society. The era of Sputnik, when education was viewed as the cornerstone of national security, is history. Funding for school districts is an annual, sometimes biannual, struggle as communities vote on school financing measures. Restrictions on funding bases fail to meet inflationary costs, so even when ballot measures are passed the funding is inadequate to sustain existing programs. Guess which programs are at the top of the hit list when cuts are required? You have it—health and physical education.

Society in general is failing in its responsibility to ensure an enlightened citizenry. This Jeffersonian principle is no less essential to a democratic society today than it was when this nation was founded. I submit it is more essential today as we compete economically and intellectually with a more enlightened *world*. The threats of a Russian Sputnik pale in comparison to the threats of the Japanese microchip! Our society has failed to recognize the threat, and the only response that can meet it, an investment both philosophically and fiscally in our system of public education.

Particularly troubling to me is a fundamental demographic that further threatens our social commitment to public education. I speak of our "graying society," a growing public that sees health care, social security, housing for the elderly, and lower taxes as priorities. These are real concerns, each competing with school financing for tax dollars. Somehow we must convince society that support of public education is an investment that is essential if we are to ensure economic vitality, an economic vitality that will provide the financial return to meet health care needs, social security, affordable housing, and lower taxes! There is a fundamental truth to the observation, if you think education is expensive, try ignorance.

What is the educational community's responsibility in this social mosaic? Our history is not a proud one. Our legacy is one of minimal academic preparation and continuing education. The old saw, "Those who can, do; those who can't, teach," is not without some basis in fact. While we have progressed over the course of this century from a 2-year undergraduate preparation for the teacher in public education to a 4-year baccalaureate degree, our standards and requirements are not impressive.

We continue to attract, on average, students with the lowest academic grade point average, SAT scores, et cetera, among the undergraduate population. The standard GPA requirement for admission to most professional education programs is a 2.50 (C+). A significant number of graduates of teacher education cannot pass an examination of basic reading, writing, and mathematical skills. In the state of Oregon this basic examination is the California Basic Educational Skills Test (CBEST), which was developed by the Education Testing Service (1988). What other profession provides financial bribes to induce continuing education? Salary increments are the carrots for taking postbaccalaureate coursework, frequently with little concern for the content and relevance. If it has an ED or PED prefix, it flies!

Overcoming this history, changing our image, will not be an easy task. But we do have an opportunity, at least in the state of Oregon, to take a major step forward. We have the opportunity—actually it's a mandate from our state legislators—to enhance the academic preparation of the teachers of tomorrow. The basic proposal is relatively simple: the elimination of all undergraduate programs in education. Students will receive a baccalaureate degree in an academic major such as mathematics, biology, human movement/kinesiology, history, or some other area. Requiring an academic major will help ensure subject matter competence and the potential for attracting some of the better students into the profession.

Eliminating the requirement of a baccalaureate degree in education will also attract potential teachers from the private sector—individuals with an intrinsic motivation toward education—further enriching the professional milieu of our public schools. The academic standards of the major will be established by a discipline-based faculty, furthering public confidence in the preparation of future teachers. In my view, a positive public perception of the educational establishment is fundamental to the solution of the many issues facing public education. Only from a base of public confidence can we effectively argue for improved salaries for professionals, for the educational equipment and facilities required for a first-rate education, and for tax bases that will support our public schools.

I have not become so enamored with the disciplinary base and the subject matter content that I have forgotten the art, the pedagogy of education. We must appreciate and provide for the teaching methodology essential for effective teaching along with opportunities to experience and apply the pedagogy of education. That ought to be the focus of the extended program, the 5th year. With an established background in the subject matter we can more effectively address the issues of classroom management, learning theories, and growth and development. We now have a relevant context that gives these important subject areas added significance.

My extended preparation model would also include a significant experiential and practice component. Opportunities would be provided during the baccalaureate program for observation and limited practice in a teaching environment. Pluralistic experiences would be encouraged. A major internship would be a capstone of the 5th year. A temporary teaching certificate would be granted only after a full year of teaching under the supervision of a master teacher to assess teaching effectiveness.

In my view, effective teaching is the capacity to establish an environment that nurtures learning so that the student can acquire information and knowledge. There needs to be evidence that learning is an outcome of the educational experience whether the setting is the classroom or the gymnasium. Having a knowledge base and an understanding of the pedagogy of the discipline does not ensure effective teaching. This can only be assessed by the outcome of the experience—the learning that takes place. There is growing evidence that successful student teaching experience (as evidenced by high school student teaching ratings) does not have a strong correlation with high academic achievement by students of these teachers (Schalock & Myton, 1988).

A standard teaching certificate would be granted following a 3-year period of *successful* and *independent* teaching. Unreasonable, unrealistic, unnecessary you say? That's what they said about the reforms proposed for the medical profession in the Flexner Report in 1910 (O'Malley, 1970). I say they are appropriate—

essential if we are to establish the academic credibility to create public confidence and influence public support for education. To do less would be to fail in our responsibility as educators, failing to provide the education necessary for our students and our society to compete successfully in the 21st century!

In summary, the elements I find essential to an effective teacher preparation model are the following:

1. There should be appreciation by our publics—parents, taxpayers, elected officials, and public institutions—that education is vital to the health and well-being of our society, and a recognition that it is an investment in our economic development as well as our intellectual and cultural development.

2. There should be a concerted effort to attract to the profession the most dedicated, compassionate, and brightest students that we can. We must shed the cloak of mediocrity, and I would suggest we start at the personal level; we must not think of ourselves as second-class citizens.

3. We must immerse these students into an educational environment that will challenge their intellect, reinforce their compassion, and temper their dedication to teaching. Essential to the experience is a solid grounding in the subject matter they will teach, followed by experiences that will help them understand the dynamics of growth and development along with the pedagogy associated with teaching. Sprinkled throughout this academic training must be hands-on experiences in the classroom and the gymnasium providing the practical knowledge essential to effective teaching. The formal training must include a capstoning experience, student teaching, that puts to the test both the personal and professional qualities of the potential teacher.

4. For those who meet the challenges of formal preparation, there awaits the privilege of the classroom. My model would provide the fledgling teacher with the opportunity to work under the guidance of a master teacher, a full-fledged mentor who has successfully demonstrated the capacity to work with students. This experience would hone the skills of the beginning teacher, helping to ensure a future of positive experiences for the teacher and his or her students.

In my view, each of these elements is essential if we are to attain the professional status we seek, meet the expectations of our publics, and satisfy our personal needs to contribute successfully to the education and development of our students. Without each of these elements and a dedication to their fulfillment, we shall remain a nation at risk.

References

A Nation Still at Risk. (1988, May 2). *Newsweek*, pp. 59-65.

CALIFORNIA Basic Educational Skills Test. (1988). Information Bulletins, October 1988–August 1989. Clovis, CA: Educational Testing Service.

HALPERT, David. (1989, February 1). U.S. eighth-graders ranked last in math in 6-nation study. *The Oregonian*, p. A1.

HODGKINSON, H.L. (1985). All one system. Demographics of education, kindergarten through graduate school. Washington, DC: The Institute for Educational Leadership, Inc.

NATIONAL Commission on Excellence in Education. (1983). *A Nation at Risk*. Washington, DC: U.S. Government Printing Office.

O'MALLEY, C.D. (1970). *The history of medical education.* Berkeley: University of California Press.

PERPICH, R. (1989, March 10). Invest in youth today, or pay the consequences. [Editorial]. *The Oregonian*, p. B9.

SCHALOCK, D.H., & Myton, D.V. (1988). A new paradigm for teacher licensure: Oregon's demand for evidence of success in fostering learning. *Journal of Teacher Education*, **39**(6), 8-16.

Undergraduate Teacher Preparation

Daryl Siedentop
The Ohio State University

To address the Academy is a special opportunity because members represent a special audience. Although few of you are trained in or actively involved in teacher preparation, you do regularly engage in scholarly work in which evidence counts, and in which arguments informed by evidence typically carry the day. I am going to stay close to the evidenciary base about teaching and teacher preparation, moving away from it only toward the end of my remarks and, even then, presenting arguments that I believe derive from the evidence.

Let me say at the outset that there is no evidence I know about from which one might conclude that undergraduate teacher preparation is better or worse, by any empirical standard, than postbaccalaureate teacher preparation. Thus the members' decision to support one or the other will be based on indirect evidence, if evidence is to inform the judgment from which the decision will be made.

The Evidence for Achievement and Teaching

The comparative evidence for achievement in American schools is mixed. For the upper 5 to 10% of students we seem to do as well or better than any nation in the world. Overall, however, we do not fare nearly so well. A significant factor mitigating the dismal overall comparisons is that we keep a larger percentage of students in school longer than do school systems in most developed nations. Achievement test scores have gone up in the past decade because dropout rates have increased steadily. Many programs are now being put in place to decrease dropout rates. If they succeed, test scores will go down. But regardless of how unfair the comparisons might be, it is clear that American schools are failing to educate the lowest 30% socioeconomically, and that percentage is increasing rather than decreasing.

The recent reform literature has generally adopted a "blame the victim" strategy (Shor, 1986) in which both students and teachers are described as mediocre, higher standards are called for, arguments for excellence achieve nearly mystical status, the expanded high school curriculum is castigated, and a get-tough policy is advocated to overcome the perceived breakdown in discipline within schools. The reform literature spent almost no time or space analyzing the budget cuts that have left class sizes too large, school buildings decrepit, teaching materials old and in short supply, and aging, overworked faculties deprived of the infusion of new ideas from new teachers.

Curiously, the evidence for teaching is generally positive. Somewhere between 20 to 40% of the variance of autumn to spring achievement gains can be attributed to teaching effects. Embedded in the residual variance is the cumulative effects of previous teaching as well as a host of individual and socioeconomic factors. Characteristics of effective teaching have been identified in large-scale field studies and correlated significantly with differential achievement gain (Brophy & Good, 1986). These effective teaching strategies have been utilized as independent variables in experimental studies and have been functionally related to statistically and socially significant achievement gains (Rosenshine & Stevens, 1986).

Effective teaching does make a difference. The expansion of the research base for effective teaching and schooling over the past 25 years has been at least as strong or stronger than in the sport sciences. There now exists a body of research about effective teaching and schooling that is *the* fundamental knowledge base for teacher preparation (Smith, 1980). This knowledge base also includes an increasing number of research derived pedagogical skills, and there is evidence that these skills can be acquired in teacher education programs (Siedentop, 1986). The transfer, maintenance, and further development of these skills in the workplace conditions that exist in many schools represent a particularly difficult set of issues about which there is mixed evidence.

Previous Postbaccalaureate Movements

There is no doubt that the educational reform literature of the past decade stands firmly in support of postbaccalaureate teacher preparation. Evidence concerning the efficacy of previous efforts in postbaccalaureate teacher preparation is limited. More than 20 years ago a Master of Arts in Teaching movement was attempted. Teachers with liberal arts degrees in subject areas received the MAT degree as teacher preparation. The research on MAT graduates indicated that they most often taught in above-average suburban schools serving the children of well-educated white parents and that they stayed in the teaching work force for an average of 5 years (Clifford & Guthrie, 1988).

A number of large school systems have experimented with hiring liberal arts graduates, giving them provisional certification as they learn on the job and take education courses part time. Haberman (1984) reported that these teachers typically do not stay on the job; often they leave before the school year ends. In one school year a large midwestern city system hired 1,000 liberal arts graduates as "emergency teachers." At the end of the year only 165 remained in the classroom. Those who stayed were the "strong insensitives," precisely the kind of teacher who is least successful in promoting achievement in urban schools.

Current Rationales
for Postbaccalaureate Preparation

The arguments in the reform literature supporting postbaccalaureate teacher preparation sort into three areas: better subject matter preparation, more liberal arts coursework, and the further professionalization of teaching. It is useful to consider each of these briefly.

More Subject Matter Preparation

The reform suggestion that teachers need more subject matter preparation seems to be based on the assumption that they do not have sufficient content knowledge to teach effectively. The evidence does not support the assumption:

> A recent meta-analysis of 65 studies of science education points out the positive but low correlation between measures of subject matter competency and student achievement, and notes that the relationship only appears to be of a substantial magnitude when higher level science courses are taught. From another half dozen studies we are assured, only, that the relationships between academic knowledge and student achievement are not negative! The review by the General Accouting Office concluded that there was no evidence for a consistent relationship between teachers' knowledge of subject matter and student achievement. The review by Everston, Hawley, and Zlotnik (1984) concludes with the most reasonable interpretation of the data: "Knowing one's subject does not necessarily make one a good teacher of that subject." (Berliner, 1985, p. 5)

The fact is that education students in most universities now take as many subject matter courses in their content field as do majors in those fields.

More Liberal Arts Preparation

Virtually every education reform document calls for more liberal arts courses for future teachers. One main reason for the move toward postbaccalaureate teacher preparation is that a thorough liberal arts preparation and an academic major take up most of the 4 years devoted to the baccalaureate. It is in examining this suggestion for more liberal arts that one can begin to see what I believe are the real agendas of the teacher education reform movement—those that are politically rather than educationally substantive.

Why more liberal arts? Look at it this way. If more liberal arts is the answer, what is the question (Shor, 1986)? I think the question is this: Why are American teachers so uncritical, so nonreflective, so conformist, and so marginally intellectual? The answer in the reform literature seems to be, They are not liberally educated—they have taken too many of those "soft" education courses and too few of those difficult, challenging liberal arts courses. Of all the arguments in the recent debate about teacher education, this one has to be the most mindless and, at the same time, the most cynical.

Does anyone believe that 20 or 30 or 40 more credit hours of the kind of traditional liberal arts coursework that is available in most of our universities will somehow transform prospective teachers who do not manifest those liberal characteristics when they enter the university? No, this version of "great books for prospective teachers" is quite simply a ploy to reduce the number of education hours students can take. At least in states like Texas, the antieducation bias is front and center, and when they wanted to reduce the number of education hours a student could accumulate, they simply mandated it directly.

Most of the emerging postbaccalaureate teacher preparation models that are designed based on these liberal arts and subject matter preparation assumptions are minimalist in nature and rely strongly on proposed internships and apprentice experiences. Why has it happened this way? Has teacher preparation been so unsuccessful at the undergraduate level?

I don't believe that the real agenda of teacher education reform is to be found in evidence about academic performance in schools or the preparation of teachers. To understand what has happened, you have to know the historic social composition of the American teaching force and how that interacts with current moves toward further professionalization of that teaching force.

The Argument for Professionalization

The seminal reference for the research related to this agenda is the Lanier and Little (1986) chapter entitled "Research on Teacher Education" that appeared in the *Third Handbook of Research on Teaching*. I believe that understanding the evidence presented in that chapter is fundamental to understanding the Holmes movement and the professionalization agenda in teacher reform.

Lanier and Little presented clear evidence that the social class origin of teacher educators and teachers has been predominantly lower middle class. While some of the best and brightest have come into teaching (typically staying a short time before moving on to their "real" work), the historic "problem," they argue, has been that too large a proportion of the teaching force have been what they describe as "lows."

In their review, Lanier and Little catalog thoroughly what research suggests has been the consequences of this historic dominance of lows in the teacher education and teaching force. Such persons are more conservative, likely to be authoritarian, restricted in their cognitive development, less analytical, more other-directed, less flexible, and conformist in their values. The picture painted by Lanier and Little is so pervasive and so apparently counterproductive to the education of children and youth that one can readily understand why, at the outset of the chapter, they simply set aside the conventional research on teacher education as uninspiring and unimportant. Yes, they admit, teaching skills can be learned by teacher candidates. Surely interns can be helped to change their attitudes and dispositions. But, they argue, these changes are unimportant when seen against the backdrop of the pervasive problems attributable to the lower middle class child-rearing and socialization of teacher educators and teacher candidates. The basic message of the chapter seems to be, You can't make a silk purse from a sow's ear!

All recent demographic data tend to exacerbate this historic problem. An increasing majority of teacher candidates come from homes where parents are skilled and unskilled workers, or clerical, sales, and farm workers (Lanier & Little, 1986, p. 538). Their academic abilities too are increasingly in question. Although measures of central tendency fall below the norm of all college students, it is the particular variance of the teacher education student population that is the problem. An increasingly large number of low achieving students have been admitted to and successfully completed education baccalaureates.

How then does one go about changing this scenario—assuming, as I think Lanier and Little did, that the appropriate conclusion is the straightforward one, namely that teacher education, teaching, and schooling will not improve as long as they are dominated by lower middle class mentalities and sensibilities, with far too many academically untalented teachers. If the conclusion is the straightforward one, then surely the solution seems to be straightforward also! To really make a difference in teaching and schooling, a larger share of academically talented teacher candidates must be recruited, and the large pool of academically inferior teacher candidates must be eliminated. And although they do not say so directly, it seems to follow that the social class origins of the teaching force must change. But how does one accomplish such a task? The answer to that question isn't found in the Lanier and Little chapter. But I think you can begin to find it in the report of the Holmes Group (1986) entitled ''Tomorrow's Teachers,'' authored, curiously enough, on behalf of the Holmes Group by their chairwoman, Judith Lanier.

To change the quality of (and I think implicitly the social class origins of) the American teaching force, one has to restrict access, provide higher standards of entry, and substantially increase the monetary rewards for work. Restricting access and providing higher standards of entry are easy to do: you simply move the preparation from the undergraduate to the graduate level. Not only can you utilize the formal standards of entry common to graduate education but you can also make teacher preparation less attractive to lower middle class and less academically talented aspirants, who typically have fewer resources to extend their education, who tend to be more instrumental and immediate in their views of the relationship between education and work, and who are less likely than their upper middle class counterparts to persevere through to a postbaccalaureate certification.

Although this might reduce access and allow for higher entry standards, it does not in and of itself guarantee the third requisite factor in the reform agenda, substantially increased financial gain for membership in the profession. Curiously, the basic plan for restructuring the teacher work force that would accomplish this last part of the puzzle has been proclaimed openly but, for some reason, not seriously attended to or debated within or outside of education.

The restructuring plan goes as follows (Shanker, 1985): To attract and retain the kind of person envisaged by the reformers as tomorrow's teacher, salaries of $80,000–90,000 will be necessary. But it is clear that no major new input of resources for education will be available. An impasse? No, it is an impasse only if you continue to view the structure of the teaching work force as it is currently constituted.

The restructing plan requires that the number of career teachers in the work force be seriously reduced. There are now about 2,000,000 teachers in the teaching work force. This number would be reduced by about two thirds (Shanker, 1985, p. 23). In the restructured model, career teachers would perform the primary educational functions of diagnosis and treatment prognosis. I use the terms advisedly. This is clearly a medical model.

The day-to-day, direct provision of educational services to children and youth would be the responsibility of a host of temporarily licenced teachers, paraprofessionals, and aides, all of whom would work for wages substantially lower than a beginning certified teacher now receives. This too would emulate the manner in which the provision of medical services has evolved over the past half century.

The higher salaries and differentiated roles for career teachers would attract academically talented teacher candidates. I think it a fair guess that a large proportion of those attracted would be sons and daughters of the professional and managerial classes. Their beginning license would come along with a master's degree. Their permanent certification would accompany something like a doctorate. These teacher candidates would be prepared in Holmes type models, mostly in research universities.

The Social Consequences of Change

That, in my judgment, represents the real agenda of teacher education reform and the salient evidence on which it is based. The Holmes model and other post-baccalaureate efforts represent a minimalist approach to teacher education. They undervalue pedagogy and overvalue subject matter competence in ways that conflict directly with research evidence related to achievement in schools. They place extraordinary confidence in an ill defined apprenticeship model, which again places belief or hope ahead of research evidence.

How will teachers prepared in this stronger liberal arts, more-subject-matter, and less pedagogy model perform in American schools as we approach the year 2000? Whatever your prediction might be, it ought to be made within the context of what those schools will be like. Here are a few salient demographic characteristics that will define American schools in the year 2000:

- One third of the students will be black or Hispanic.
- One sixth of the students will be children of a teenage mother and more than three fourths of those mothers will be unwed.
- One fourth of the children (one half if black) will be from families whose income falls below the federal poverty line.
- In urban schools, more than three fourths of the students will be minorities.
- Dropout rates from urban schools are likely to reach 40-45%; unemployment of minority students who do not drop out will remain above 50%.
- We will be spending progressively less on urban schools and more on their suburban counterparts, a trend that has persisted for 20 years.
- Students in American schools will be increasingly less likely to learn from a minority teacher.
- In urban schools, nearly one third of all classes will be taught by a teacher not certified in that subject.

How will tomorrow's teachers fare in tomorrow's schools? Not well, I predict, especially in urban schools. All evidence suggests that failures in teaching derive from a lack of pedagogical skill rather than inadequate subject matter knowledge. If we viewed the crisis in education as primarily social rather than economic, as an expression of social inequality, then we would be examining very different models. Undergraduate teacher education would be strengthened rather than weakened. The knowledge base for teaching would receive more rather than fewer credit hours. Access for minority candidates would be made more rather than less attractive. But that represents a different agenda.

The recent reform movement is the logical extension of neoconservative policy to education, with its goal of improving America's international economic position and its vision of the deregulated school system through which that goal will be achieved. That there is a widening gulf in our nation between those who have and those who have not is indisputable. If we continue on our present course of educational reform, we will ensure that the school system becomes a primay means by which those differences are maintained and increased in the future.

References

BERLINER, D. (1985). *Reform in teacher education: The case for pedagogy* (Occasional paper No. 1). Association for Colleges and Schools of Education and Land Grant Colleges and Affiliated Private Universities.

BROPHY, J., & Good, T. (1986). Teacher behavior and student achievement. In M. Wittrock (Ed.), *Handbook of research on teaching* (3rd ed.) (pp. 328-375). New York: Macmillan.

CLIFFORD, J.C., & Guthrie, J.W. (1988). *Ed school.* Chicago: University of Chicago Press.

HABERMAN, M. (1984). *An evaluation of the rationale for required teacher education: Beginning teachers with and without teacher preparation.* Paper prepared for the National Commission on Excellence in Teacher Education. (Available from M. Haberman, Division of Urban Outreach, University of Wisconsin-Milwaukee)

HOLMES Group Report, The. *Tomorrow's teachers: A report of the Holmes Group.* (1986). East Lansing, MI: Holmes Group, Inc.

LANIER, J., & Little, J. (1986). Research on teacher education. In M. Wittrock (Ed.), *Handbook of research on teaching* (3rd ed.) (pp. 527-569). New York: Macmillan.

ROSENSHINE, B., & Stevens, R. (1986). Teaching functions. In M. Wittrock (Ed.), *Handbook of research on teaching* (3rd ed.) (pp. 376-391). New York: Macmillan.

SHANKER, A. (1985). *The making of a profession.* Washington, DC: American Federation of Teachers.

SHOR, I. (1986). Equality is excellence: Transforming teacher education and the learning process. *Harvard Educational Review*, **56**(4), 406-426.

SIEDENTOP, D. (1986). The modification of teacher behavior. In M. Piéron & G. Graham (Eds.), *Sport pedagogy* (pp. 3-18). Champaign, IL: Human Kinetics.

SMITH, B.O. (1980). *Design for a school of pedagogy.* Washington, DC: U.S. Department of Education.

The Name Game:
Power and Turf at the 61st Meeting

Lawrence F. Locke
University of Massachusetts

The two papers you have just heard will speak for themselves. They need no translation, no clarification, and no further elucidation. Each can stand on its own—what you heard is what you have. They tell us about alternatives for configuring teacher preparation, and they provide some analysis of the motives that others, and we ourselves, might have for adopting particular arrangements of content and timing in programs leading to teacher certification.

The foregoing, however, were only parts of a program, 2 days of papers with reactions and discussions, all ostensibly about the same theme. What was said here is intended to contribute to what we learned from the previous discussion of ''the body of knowledge,'' and what we will learn from tomorrow's discussion of ''the name.'' In short, what Siedentop and Maksud have said must take its meaning from the context provided by the other 11 speakers on the program.

That being the case, we can best appreciate those two papers by framing them within a correct understanding of what it is we are talking about at this 61st meeting of the Academy. President-Elect Corbin, as program chair, set the topic for us—''The Evolving Undergraduate Major.'' That is the title Professor Park, our historian, will record in the archives, and that is the title Professor Eckert will use as she compiles these *Academy Papers*. Both of those sources will serve to sorely puzzle future generations of graduate students assigned the task of reading our corporate record, however, because the undergraduate major, evolving or otherwise, is distinctly not what we are talking about.

In genteel company, giving a name to what is going on often is unwelcome and sometimes is embarrassing to everyone. For example, when you have invited your extended family to a formal sit-down dinner, and a visiting aunt or uncle has a momentary problem with sphincter control, leading your youngest to observe in an enthusiastic voice, ''Uncle Charley just farted!'' it takes a parent with unusual equanimity to say, ''That's nice dear.'' However mortifying the event, it is not the parent's perception but the child's eye, or in this case, ear, that is the honest one. Fortunately, that also is something that kindly uncles and aunts, in their wisdom, both understand and love.

Hoping you will remember that same kind of affectionate charity, I now will embarrass us all by noticing what we really are talking about. This program

35

is about *power* and *turf*. It is about who will control the undergraduate major, not about what is in it or its present state of evolution. This program is about who will teach it and which students will be required to take it. We are talking about a test of the political power produced by a new alliance between the disciplinarians and the neoconservative ideology of the educational reform movement. We are asking ourselves, one more time, whether the faculty who teach academic courses in physical education now have the capability to control the life space— credits, content, programs of study, and resources—of the undergraduate program.

What we are talking about has little to do with the subject matter of physical education, which I take to be sports, games, dance, and exercise, the forms of motoric play. What we are talking about has even less to do with the real knowledge base for teacher education, which I take to be the fruits of systematic inquiry into teachers, teaching, learning to teach, educational programs, and contexts for instruction. Our dialogues, like many of those going on in state legislatures across the nation, will not even mention the problems of delivering high quality education to our client populations in the public schools. All such talk will be assiduously avoided while we pretend to be discussing "the evolving undergraduate major."

Anyone who was present 12 years ago in Orlando for the historic first joint meeting of the men's and women's college associations is here permitted a moment of a déjà vu. Then too, we had both an ostensible program and a real agenda. Elegantly orchestrated by Bob Morford, that Florida meeting marked the cresting of the first wave of the disciplines movement in physical education.

The disciples from Berkeley were young, energetic, imbued with the fire of true-believership, and they had two grave problems. First, they needed "life space" in which to flourish and grow, space that was hard to come by in a time of declining resources. Second, they were embarrassed by their association, through teacher education, with schools, children, the frivolity of play, the taints of college athletics, and worse, colleges of education.

In the heady academic communities to which the disciplinarians aspired, it did not pay to have too many poor cousins. Then, as now, the war cry was "Change the name to something with respectability!" and the agenda included either reorganizing to make work with teachers a well-concealed subsidiary enterprise in an otherwise academically pure administrative unit or, better yet, to move the embarrassing cousins out of the homestead altogether.

Proud of our colleagues and their achievements, many of us urged realistic accommodation. In some institutions, and certainly in our national organizations, compromises gave the disciplinarians a share of the loaf they desired. In the main, however, their reach exceeded their grasp and the momentum of the moment was lost.

Through the long subsequent winter of their discontent, our colleagues have been industrious and ever watchful for new opportunity. Strengthened by continuing academic achievements and by the growth of ancillary programs such as sport management and health related services, the disciplinarians now are older, more experienced, no less energetic, just as certain that the tide of history runs in their favor, and still convinced that teacher education is a drag on progress toward their destiny.

This time, in 1989, however, there is a new factor. The work of preparing teachers and nuturing practitioners has changed dramatically. Neither the people nor the processes are what they were. A generation has passed and now it is teacher education that has the burgeoning body of knowledge. Now it is teacher education that is restless in its cramped confines and seeking new, wider, life space. Decisions about content and process in teacher education no longer are made by generalists and academics. With the exception of rare, isolationist pockets of reactionism, control of preparation curriculum has everywhere been made the responsibility of a new kind of specialist—the teacher educators.

The inevitable collision of interests is upon us. The only thing that can surprise anyone is that the disciplinarians seem unaware anything has changed since 1976. The design of this morning's program, which inadvertently (I will charitably assume) excluded the most rapidly growing and exciting field of inquiry in physical education, is evidence of the degree to which the disciplinarians are out of touch with real events. To title this session on professional programs "Beyond the Body of Knowledge," however, required a degree of arrogance that is not easily excused by ignorance.

But we should be civil and not talk in parables or about imaginary groups engaged in mythic contests. Let us just name what we have here. A teacher preparation model in which learning how to teach is neatly tucked away into a postbaccalaureate 5th year would mean that the annual cadres of undergraduates destined for careers in teaching—now, if Siedentop's analysis is correct, safely all-white, monolingual, middle class, and above the mystical SAT cut score—would need an undergraduate major appropriate to their vocational ambitions.

Surely not just any liberal arts or science curriculum would do. We ask, "Any volunteers?" Guess what? The "academic discipline of kinesiology" in which the study of sports, games, dance, and exercise is done by talking about them, never by engaging in them—the academic major of kinesiology in which no attention whatever need be paid to the messy business of professional training—stands ready to raise its hand and step forward.

The disciplinarians covet those captive, credit-bearing clients who still constitute the largest single population of undergraduate students passing through most of our schools, colleges, and departments. All that is needed to accomplish the capture is to create a tidy segregation of professional preparation into another time block, being careful of course not to absorb by accident any significant responsibility for preprofessional preparation. For that, Holmes and the 5th-year model provide the perfect leverage. Then, by cunningly renaming the enterprise so as to exclude any disruptive representation of knowledge from pedagogy and curriculum, the entire package is secured.

As President Spirduso has observed on every possible occasion during the past year, she believes it essential that our name give exactly the right signal, most notably that we no longer deal with children and education but have become purified, worthy of membership in the sacred inner circle of liberal and scientific studies. That, for our disciplinary colleagues, is the consummation devoutly to be desired. Fortunately, I think it will not come to pass.

There will be change as teacher education flexes to accommodate the evidence of new research on teaching and learning to teach. The wave of the future may turn out to be the 5-year program, not the 5th-year model. Instead of reading *Tomorrow's Teachers* (Holmes Group, 1986), the enthusiasts for kinesiology might better peruse *Educating a Profession* (Howsam, Corrigan, Denemark, & Nash, 1976) with its conclusions about the needed expansion of teacher training.

Before casting their lot with those who call for dismembering undergraduate teacher education, the disciplinarians should understand that the reform movement already is in disarray. It can provide only the most undependable guidance about what will happen in the future. This is partly because the people involved have ignored the history of such efforts in the United States (Bush, 1987; Keith, 1987; Warren, 1985). One specialist on reform issues observed that top-down reform movements have a perfect record—not one has ever succeeded (Cornbleth, 1986).

The disarray arises also from being just plain wrong, a consequence of ignoring research evidence about what works and what does not work in training teachers (Ashton & Crocker, 1987; Evertson, Hawley, & Zlotnik, 1985). Finally, at the bottom line, the reform movement is a political phenomenon led by opportunists who, having no genuine or persisting interest in education, want only to appear to have done something to resolve our national malaise concerning public schools—without of course raising taxes. That bit of illusion created, most of them will move on to more fertile pastures for demagoguery.

The list of wounded and missing among the reformers is depressing. *A Nation at Risk* (National Commission on Excellence in Education, 1983) now is regarded as an embarrassment even among neoconservatives. *A Nation Prepared* (Carnegie Task Force on Teaching as a Profession, 1986) was stillborn as a serious proposal for action, which shows that grand rhetoric and big money still do not purchase the moral authority to lead in education. The Holmes Group is desperately maneuvering to avoid total collapse. Underfunded, overextended, arrogant, riddled with dissention, and now co-opted by ambitious state legislatures, *Tomorrow's Teachers* (Holmes Group, 1986) may prove in most state institutions to be more of a liability than an asset.

Indeed, the spectacle of blue ribbon committees populated by Wall Street brokers, savings and loan presidents, and oil company CEOs presuming to lecture us on accountability, integrity, and how to run the schools properly has come back to haunt the reform movement. Reforming teacher education by exhortation or by punitive legislation is a snare and a delusion, if detectable improvement is held as the test of success.

Nevertheless, options for repackaging are real and require honest appraisal. What is clear from the proceeding papers, however, is that the choice will be neither simple nor obvious. As Siedentop observed, there is no particular magic in either 4-year or postgraduate models. Certainly it is not impossible to imagine a workable program at the master's level. At the least, such programs offer the advantage of working with a more mature population. As anyone who has taught in a MAT program will tell you, it is a comparative delight to work with people who already have resolved the great earthy questions of adolescence.

The problem with most 5th-year models is that they are thinly veiled attempts to put teacher education in a Procrustean bed. Most versions of the Holmes plan attempt to cram a major practicum and the requisite continuation of academic study into the credit equivalent of a master's degree. That leaves almost no time for serious teacher preparation. Even plans employing a calendar year rather than an academic year involve reductions in the inadequate time now available in most 4-year programs.

Based on what I have learned from our program at UMass, to do what we know has to be accomplished demands not less than three semesters of full-time study plus an additional semester of an intensively supervised, full-time, clinical practicum. That adds up to 2 academic years. Even then, what can be accomplished does no more than make a graduate minimally safe to work with children and begin the long process of becoming a teacher.

If the size of the box were the only issue, 2-year postgraduate programs would be fine. Unfortunately, as the Siedentop paper notes, they serve to compound all the negative social consequences that attend any significant extension of preparation beyond the 4-year model. The clear options of choice are either a 5-year plan or a reformulated undergraduate major that puts the study of teaching and the subject matter at the center of the curriculum. The latter choice has some stringent consequences. A major that focused on doing sport, dance, and exercise in context with the examination of their teachability—what Shulman calls pedagogical subject matter knowledge (Shulman, 1987)—would require the virtual elimination of the disciplinary foundation courses, at least as they presently are taught.

If 5th-year plans present notable disadvantages for teacher educators (and they do), and new 4-year plans have clear risks for the disciplines (and they will), a commonsense compromise that serves the interests of all might not be difficult to locate. What is required of course is a willingness to listen and learn from each other, behaviors that have not characterized many of our exchanges in the past.

Certainly the disciplinarians are quite correct in their obvious conclusion that this is a moment of flux in teacher education—the ideal time to induce change. Social circumstances and a growing knowledge base together provide a marvelous opportunity to gain ground on the old problems of preparing teachers.

Two decades of energetic study have taught us a great deal about effective teaching. An as yet young effort to study how teachers learn and what it is that expert teachers really know and do has begun to yield some surprising and potentially powerful results. Among them are indications that there may even be ways to make disciplinary study useful in the work of giving instruction. For a provocative example, you might consult some of the recent dissertations on pedagogical kinesiology (Siedentop, 1989).

The possibility of bridges between disciplines and profession suggests partnerships in which common interests are identified and pursued. It suggests sharing rather than contesting programmatic turf. It may be, however, that the political realities of our situation make collaboration impossible. We may have created a zero-sum game from which neither side can retreat.

I hope this is not true. If either side were to truly win, all of us would truly lose. A small move toward peace would do this Academy great credit.

Addendum

It was here that this paper was to end. I had planned to say "*pax vobiscum*" and sit down. There is now, however, a short coda. It is a tradition at UMass to test our public utterances on each other, and I did so with what you have just heard. At a convenient seminar, my trial audience did not fall asleep or make rude noises, but at the benediction there was a long silence and the telltale shuffling of papers.

I asked, "Well, what's the problem?" After a pause, a particularly precocious graduate student said, "We can't tell what it is that you really want." Mystified, I asked what that meant. Came the answer, "From what you said, nobody will know whether you are drawing a line in the dirt and warning the disciplinarians to back off, or you're wimping out and offering them the whole farm if they'll just stop picking on you." That got my attention. Some reflection indicated that the graduate students were right. I have a responsibility to say exactly what I want.

There should be no name change for the Academy. This organization is not ours. We hold it only in trust for others. While the thousands of people whose education and careers made it possible for all of us to be here still call what they do "physical education," we dare not betray that trust.

As for the naming of other organizations, institutions, academic majors, and disciplinary concentrations, I am willing to see the democratic process take its course, both here in Boston and elsewhere—except at UMass, where Frank Katch and I will go head to head over 10 kilometers on the Fourth of July, winner take all!

What I want for teacher education is equally clear. If there is to be reorganization of programs, majors, degrees, and resources, then let us get on with it. In some states the legislature already has done it, or shortly will do it, for you. Where we are left to decide among ourselves, however, you must understand that we will come out of any negotiation with an arrangement that allows us to do the work of teacher preparation better. Anything short of that will be unacceptable.

If the name of the game is negotiation, then both sides establish opening positions and we start from scratch. Here is what teacher educators everywhere are likely to put on the table. The content of any major that is directly preprofessional will be determined by teacher educators and not by anyone else. If in any given institution there is an academic undergraduate major, teacher educators will determine which experiences, if any, might be useful in preparing teachers. The nature of content and instruction in any course that is selected as foundational for teacher preparation will be subject to review and development by teacher educators in collaboration with academic colleagues. That is a reasonable opening position. When the disciplinarians have laid their starting proposals on the table, we can begin.

Most of us, however, would prefer a different mode of program design, one in which the agenda is not power and turf but cooperation and the courage to envision new structure and relationships—to achieve that we will need to name the game precisely, and then play it on a level field, a condition not provided by the design of this Academy program.

References

ASHTON, P., & Crocker, L. (1987). Systematic study of planned variations: The essential focus of teacher education reform. *Journal of Teacher Education, 38*(3), 2-8.

BUSH, R.N. (1987). Teacher education reform: Lessons from the past half century. *Journal of Teacher Education, 38*(3), 13-19.

CARNEGIE Task Force on Teaching as a Profession. (1986). *A nation prepared: Teachers for the 21st century.* New York: Carnegie Forum on Education and the Economy, Carnegie Corp.

CORNBLETH, C. (1986). Ritual and rationality in teacher education reform. *Educational Researcher,* **15**(4), 5-14.

EVERTSON, C., Hawley, W., & Zlotnik, M. (1985). Making a difference in educational quality through teacher education. *Journal of Teacher Education,* **36**(3), 2-12.

HOLMES Group Report, The. Tomorrow's teachers: A report of the Holmes Group. (1986). East Lansing, MI: Holmes Group, Inc.

HOWSAM, R., Corrigan, D., Denemark, G., & Nash, R. (1976). *Educating a profession.* Washington, DC: American Association of Colleges for Teacher Education.

KEITH, M.J. (1987). We've heard this song . . . Or have we? *Journal of Teacher Education,* **38**(3), 20-25.

NATIONAL Commission on Excellence in Education. (1983). *A nation at risk: A report to the nation and the Secretary of Education.* Washington, DC: U.S. Dept. of Education.

SHULMAN, L. (1987). Knowledge and teaching: Foundations of a new reform. *Harvard Educational Review,* **57**(1), 1-22.

SIEDENTOP, D. (1989). *Skill analysis: Prerequisite for effective feedback.* Unpublished manuscript, The Ohio State University.

WARREN, D. (1985). Learning from experience: History and teacher education. *Educational Researcher,* **14**(10), 5-12.

Structure for Undergraduate Kinesiology Programs

B. Don Franks
Louisiana State University

Undergraduate education in our field has been and will continue to be influenced by numerous external factors including (a) changes in the society (such as increased numbers of older individuals, a larger percent of minorities, more women working, more frequent career changes), (b) shifts in funding for our services, (c) increased recognition of the professional application of kinesiology, (d) recommendations for educational reform at all levels, and (e) university-wide changes in general education. Others (e.g., Ellis, 1988; Hodgkinson, 1986; Oliver, 1988) have dealt with some of these factors. Other speakers in this symposium have discussed the impact of teacher-education reforms.

Changes in our undergraduate programs have occurred partly as a result of internal factors. Some of these have been within local situations; however, part of the future of our field will rely on our development of a purposeful future based on what we think should be done—not ignoring the external element, but making conscious decisions based on all pertinent factors. For example, Kretchmar (1988) and Razor (1988) call for a clearer definition of our field and its missions. I want to extend that call to recommend a process to do just that. However, first I will briefly describe some elements of our current undergraduate kinesiology programs.

This paper contains an outline of the general structure for a variety of kinesiology[1] undergraduate programs, a description of what appears to be a consensus on a kinesiology core among major research institutions, and questions that need to be addressed. I will conclude with recommendations on how the American Academy of Physical Education might facilitate resolution of these issues. Sources for the paper include a survey of undergraduate kinesiology programs in the Carnegie Foundation Research I and II institutions, a review of the recent literature, and my opinions.

Scope of Undergraduate Programs

Departments of kinesiology of the 99 Carnegie Foundation Research I and II institutions were asked to send information on their undergraduate program areas.

---

[1]I have used kinesiology as the broad name for our field. As others have documented, many different names are currently being used.

Table 1

University Programs Analyzed

Arizona State	Kansas	Purdue
Auburn	Kansas State	Rhode Island
California, Berkeley	Louisiana State	Southern California
Cincinnati	Maryland	Syracuse
Colorado	Massachusetts	Temple
Colorado State	Michigan	Tennessee
Delaware	Mississippi State	Texas A&M
Florida	Missouri	Utah
Florida State	Nebraska	Utah State
Georgia	New Mexico	Virginia
Hawaii	New Mexico State	Virginia Polytechnic
Illinois	North Carolina, CH	Washington State
Indiana	Oregon	Wayne State
Iowa	Oregon State	West Virginia
Iowa State	Pennsylvania State	Wisconsin

Sixty-three (64%) responded. Of those responding, 13 have no undergraduate major in this area; 3 sent information that could not be used. Table 1 includes the universities (*N*=45) that were used for this paper. Table 2 includes the different undergraduate tracts[2] that are currently being offered at the major research institutions. Table 2 includes professional preparation (physical education, athletic training, fitness, fitness leadership, sport management), bases for professional school (pre-physical therapy, athletic training), bases for graduate work (exercise physiology, biomechanics), and a liberal arts study of human movement (kinesiology, exercise science, sport science).

It is not surprising, given our history, that almost all universities continue to have teacher preparation. Parenthetically, let me state my strong support for school physical education, which, along with TV, is one of the few means we have of reaching all our citizens (some of our areas, such as executive fitness programs, are available only to a small percent of the population). As Schwebel (1985) pointed out and as Hellison (1986) has found, this will continue to be an uphill battle. I learned from Lawson (1980) that I should include this note to try to avoid the tar and feathers from Locke and Siedentop (1980). Because teacher education for physical educators has been covered in other parts of this program, this paper will not deal with it.

The undergraduate tracts not related to school physical education have greatly expanded during the 1980s (Bunnell, 1981; Douglas, 1979; Groves, 1979; Stier, 1986). Several persons have provided a comprehensive overview of the different areas of kinesiology (Haag, 1979; Lawson & Morford, 1979; Mawson,

---

[2]I have used the names for subareas suggested by Zeigler (1983), although many different names are currently being used for each of the undergraduate emphases and subareas of the core.

Table 2

Undergraduate Kinesiology Tracts at Research Universities (N = 45)

Tract	Number	%
Physical education	43	92
Athletic training	18	38
Fitness	18	38
Exercise science	17	36
Kinesiology (broad definition)	12	26
Sport management	11	23
Sport science	10	21
Fitness leadership	8	17
Exercise physiology	7	15
Pre-physical therapy	6	13
Biomechanics	3	6

1984; Singer, 1979; Zeigler, 1983). Others have provided recommendations for programs in specific areas, such as biomechanics (Kinesiology Academy, 1987), exercise science (Maynard & Leslie, 1988), motor behavior (Bird & Ross, 1984; Hatfield, 1984), pedagogy (Haag, 1978), sociology of sport (Hollands, 1984; Ingham, 1979), sport history (Lucas, 1979), and sport management (Lopiano, 1984; Parkhouse & Ulrich, 1979; Parks & Quain, 1986; VanderZwaag, 1983). Descriptions have often been provided of undergraduate programs in other countries (e.g., Riordan, 1979; Williams, 1979).

Undergraduate Program Structure

Undergraduate programs in our field normally include the following:
- General education (often with specific suggestions for some areas),
- Kinesiology core,
- Professional or preprofessional experiences.

Although no attempt was made to analyze the quality of the general education requirements, the possibility of a strong liberal arts base advocated by many of our leaders (e.g., Becker, 1985a) is there. There is also the provision for both the discipline and the profession (Bressan, 1979). In addition, human anatomy, human physiology, and health are commonly required general education elements for our programs.

Kinesiology Core

Some have argued for a graduate core (e.g., Thomas, 1985), but I contend that the undergraduate level is the more appropriate place for a core (with relevant prerequisites for graduate programs). There is wide agreement on a core of classes[2] that should be included for all our undergraduate programs (see Table 3), although there are numerous names and combinations for the courses. Local

Table 3

Core Areas for Kinesiology Undergraduate Programs

	Included in core	
Area	Different tracts[a] Range (%)	Average[b] %
Exercise physiology	57–100	83
Biomechanics	55–100	82
Physical activity	33–95	68
Sociology/psychology	33–81	60
Field experiences	25–88	60
Motor learning	12–100	58
History/philosophy	29–86	55
Athletic training/injury	14–100	52
Orientation	28–71	47
Fitness	10–100	45
Measurement	14–88	43
Administration	0–100	36
First aid	0–67	35
Motor development	10–67	31
Adapted physical education	0–81	30
Curriculum	0–74	21
Methods	0–86	18

[a]The range of percent of programs in each tract listed in Table 2 that include this subarea in their core. [b]The average percent that require this subarea as part of their core from tracts listed in Table 2. The average is the percent from each tract summed and divided by the number of tracts.

approaches to teaching classes may rely heavily on the parent disciplines, but having the courses in our departments can be the basis for having the study of human movement as the basis for the core (Bressan, 1982; Metheny, 1967) or, more likely, a combination of inter- and cross-disciplinary approaches (Brooks, 1981). These programs would appear to meet most of the criteria established by Clayton and Clayton (1984) for selection of a program, including more than one interdisciplinary program, with competent faculty and internship experiences. It appears that these programs will appeal to different students than the school physical education programs (Templin, Woodford, & Mulling, 1982).

Although physical activity is included as part of the core, it does not appear to have the central focus that some would advocate (Broekhoff, 1979, 1982; Metheny, 1967; Rose, 1986). Having a common core with specific professional (or preprofessional or pregraduate) experiences would allow for specialization without fragmentation (Greendorfer, 1987; Lawson, 1980; Sheehan, 1984). Having generic, preprofessional, pregraduate, and professional tracts allows us to include the constructive tensions (theory and activity, disciplinary and professional experiences, basic information and hands-on experiences) advocated by many scholars (e.g., Fraleigh, 1985; Lawson, 1979; O'Brien, 1985; O'Hanlon & Wandzilak, 1980; Sage, 1984).

In this way, the basic structure for the Holmes model applies to these tracts as well. The generic kinesiology core is analogous to a liberal arts major in another discipline (e.g., math), with pregraduate or professional experiences dependent on the individual student's future goals. The generic and pregraduate tracts can emphasize the discipline of our field, and the professional and preprofessional tracts can include the professional experiences called for by some of our scholars (Broekhoff, 1982; Ellis, 1988).

Three themes in the literature that don't seem to be directly reflected in the curriculum (although individual teachers include these in their teaching style and as a part of some courses) are (a) problem setting/solving (Bain, 1982; Lawson, 1984; Lawson & Sinclair, 1982; Miller, 1987; Wendt, 1982, 1983), (b) ethical/ moral development (Scully, 1986), and (c) inclusion of all groups (Bain, 1985; Hellison, 1986, 1987, 1988; Oliver, 1988).

Professional Experiences

There is agreement that specialized courses in our field and related disciplines and a major field experience should be included in the programs of study. We can learn about creative field experiences from our teacher-educator brothers and sisters (e.g., Anderson, 1982).

Issues

I base the rest of this paper on the assumption that there is a need for some national consensus about certain aspects of our future. I would not disagree with the point made by Berg (1988) and Lawson (1988) that there will and should always be a local flavor to our programs; however, the scope of the local options should be smaller than the current case, in my opinion. A resolution of the following issues at the national level would benefit our field:

- What is the best name for the different program emphases?
- What are the essential components of each of the subareas?
- What is the best name for each of the subareas of the core?
- How can the 4-year, 5-year, and master's programs be clearly described and differentiated?

Program Emphases and Subareas

Table 2 included the current tracts offered in our field. The specific names given these tracts vary among universities. I believe we should set up a process to arrive at common names for these areas.

Most of the programs are set up on a 4-year basis; however, it is a common observation that many of the programs (especially the professional ones) are normally completed in more than 4 years. The major additional element of the professional preparation programs is an intensive intern experience. I believe that a logical recommendation for 4- and 5-year programs is that the 4-year program include generic, preprofessional, and pregraduate study, and the 5-year program the professional preparation. In a similar way, master's programs can be divided into those that are professional preparation (for entry into the profession at a higher level) and predoctoral study. We need more definition of what experiences will be essential and helpful for professional practice, professional schools, and graduate study (e.g., Becker, 1985b; Bryant, 1985).

Relation to Other Fields

I have alluded to encouragement of our students to take courses in health and fields related to their professional interests (e.g., business for sport management). There are obvious links between some of our program emphases and dance, health, and leisure studies. Several universities have joint programs in one or more areas. These joint programs seem to be based more on the particular individuals in the different fields and the local scope of the administrative unit than on any broad-based consensus or logic. Although I believe there are some natural alliances that should be expanded, I am not confident that this issue can approach a nation-wide solution at this time. I am therefore suggesting a more provincial approach with an emphasis on getting our own kinesiology house in order, realizing that the links to dance, health, or leisure will take place in the unique local context.

Specific Recommendations

The basic thesis for my recommendations is that we have gone beyond the point where a leader of the field can provide the basis for a consensus (e.g., Henry, 1964), or a leading institution can describe what it has done and that will become the basis for the consensus (e.g., Bird, 1988; Vincent, Winningham, & Cald-well, 1988). I do believe that we can make some progress in common names and competencies for our program emphases and subareas. I recommend that the AAPE facilitate this progress by asking the National Association for Physical Education in Higher Education (NAPEHE); the groups in the Exercise/Sport Network (ESN); the American Alliance for Health, Physical Education, Recreation and Dance (AAHPERD); and the Academies in the National Association for Sport and Physical Education (NASPE) (ensuring that we have curriculum theorists [Jewett, 1980, 1986], futurists [Robinson, 1980], and professionals in various fields [Anderson, 1988]) to join together to reach consensus on the following issues to be published by 1995: (a) a name and definition for each program emphasis in our field, (b) the concepts that should be included in each subarea in our undergraduate core, and (c) a name and definition for each subarea. The following timetable is recommended:

- 1990—Get these items on the agenda for ESN and its member groups, including AAPE, NAPEHE, and NASPE Academies,
- 1992—Hold pre-AAPE working workshop,
- 1993—Issue position statement widely distributed for feedback,
- 1994—Hold pre-AAPE writing conference,
- 1995—Publish consensus.

I don't believe that arriving at common names and definitions is the most important issue for our field; however, I do think the kind of process used and the resulting consensus on labels can provide the basis for more important issues. For example, the next steps would include a strategy for influencing institutions, organizations, and periodicals to use common language. Questions concerning evaluation (Loughery, 1985, 1987; Scahill, 1988) and standards for higher quality programs (Bucker, 1982; Douglas & Wiegand, 1987; Lawson, 1985; Oberle, 1988) could be more adequately addressed using common names and definitions.

References

ANDERSON, W.G. (1982). A physical education program development center. *Journal of Physical Education, Recreation and Dance*, **53**(5), 7-10.

ANDERSON, W.G. (1988). Preparing and using the written curriculum. *Journal of Physical Education, Recreation and Dance*, **59**(2), 67-72.

BAIN, L.L. (1982). Preparing students for the future: Developing change agent skills. *National Association for Physical Education in Higher Education Proceedings*, **3**, 101-106.

BAIN, L.L. (1985). The hidden curriculum re-examined. *Quest*, **37**(2), 145-153.

BECKER, B.J. (1985a). The long green line. *Quest*, **37**, 128-133.

BECKER, B.J. (1985b). Undergraduate education for graduate study. *National Association for Physical Education in Higher Education Proceedings*, **6**, 67-71.

BERG, K. (1988). A national curriculum. *Journal of Physical Education, Recreation and Dance*, **59**(9), 70-75.

BIRD, A.M., & Ross, D. (1984). Current methodological problems and future directions for theory development in the psychology of sport and motor behavior. *Quest*, **36**, 1-6.

BIRD, P.J. (1988). College name change: A rationale. *Journal of Physical Education, Recreation and Dance*, **59**(1), 25-27.

BRESSAN, E.S. (1979). 2001: The profession is dead—Was it murder or suicide? *Quest*, **31**, 77-82.

BRESSAN, E.S. (1982). An academic discipline for physical education: What a fine mess? *National Association for Physical Education in Higher Education Proceedings*, **3**, 22-27.

BROEKHOFF, J. (1979). Physical education as a profession. *Quest*, **31**(2), 244-254.

BROEKHOFF, J. (1982). A discipline—who needs it. *Proceedings of National Association of Physical Education in Higher Education*, **3**, 28-36.

BROOKS, G.A. (1981). What is the discipline of physical education? In G.A. Brooks (Ed.), *Perspectives on the academic discipline of physical education*. Champaign, IL: Human Kinetics.

BRYANT, J.E. (1985). The undergraduate program for admission to graduate study. *National Association for Physical Education in Higher Education Proceedings*, **6**, 64-66.

BUCKER, C.A. (1982). The future of physical education and sport. *Journal of Physical Education, Recreation and Dance*, **53**, 12-14.

BUNNELL, R.D. (1981). Major and minor programs in health, physical education, and recreation. *Journal of Physical Education, Recreation and Dance*, **52**(3), 62-64.

CLAYTON, R.D., & Clayton, J.A. (1984). Careers and professional preparation programs. *Journal of Physical Education, Recreation and Dance*, **55**(5), 44-45.

DOUGLAS, J.W. (1979). Assessment of alternative career curricula at four-year colleges and universities. *Journal of Physical Education, Recreation and Dance*, **50**(5), 66-68.

DOUGLAS, J.W., & Wiegand, R.L. (1987). NCATE evaluation: Preparing physical education teacher educators. *Journal of Physical Education, Recreation and Dance*, **58**(1), 67-69.

ELLIS, M.J. (1988). Warning: The pendulum has swung far enough. *Journal of Physical Education, Recreation and Dance*, **59**(3), 75-78.

FRALEIGH, W.P. (1985). Unresolved tensions in college physical education—Constructive and destructive. *Quest*, **37**, 135-144.

GREENDORFER, S.L. (1987). Specialization, fragmentation, integration, discipline, profession: What is the real issue? *Quest*, **39**(1), 56-64.

GROVES, R. (1979). Career options within the undergraduate major. *Journal of Physical Education, Recreation and Dance*, **50**(6), 84.

HAAG, H. (1978). *Sport pedagogy: Content and methodology*. Baltimore: University Park Press.

HAAG, H. (1979). Development and structure of a theoretical framework for sport science ("sportwissenschaft"). *Quest*, **31**(1), 25-35.

HATFIELD, B.D. (1984). Psychological knowledge and its emerging role in the physical education curriculum. *National Association for Physical Education in Higher Education Proceedings*, **5**, 60-68.

HELLISON, D. (1986). Professional priorities. *Journal of Physical Education, Recreation and Dance*, **56**(7), 33-34.

HELLISON, D. (1987). The affective domain in physical education: Let's do some housecleaning. *Journal of Physical Education, Recreation and Dance*, **56**, 41-43.

HELLISON, D. (1988). Cause of death: Physical education—A sequel. *Journal of Physical Education, Recreation and Dance*, **59**(4), 18-21.

HENRY, F.M. (1964). Physical education: An academic discipline. *Journal of Health, Physical Education and Recreation*, **35**, 32-33; 69.

HODGKINSON, H.L. (1986). Reform? Higher education? Don't be absurd. *Phi Delta Kappan*, **68**(4), 271-274.

HOLLANDS, R.G. (1984). The role of cultural studies and social criticism in the sociological study of sport. *Quest*, **36**(1), 66-79.

INGHAM, A.G. (1979). Methodology in the sociology of sport: From symptoms of malaise to Weber for a cure. *Quest*, **31**(2), 187-215.

JEWETT, A.E. (1980). The status of physical education curriculum theory. *Quest*, **32**(2), 163-173.

JEWETT, A.E. (1986). Happenings of the fifth order: The cutting edge in curriculum research. *The Academy Papers. The Cutting Edge in Physical Education and Exercise Science Research* (No. 20, pp. 70-82). Champaign, IL: Human Kinetics.

KINESIOLOGY Academy. (1987). Guidelines for the undergraduate preparation of teachers in physical education. *Journal of Physical Education, Recreation and Dance*, **58**(1), 70-71.

KRETCHMAR, R.S. (1988). Toward a stronger position for physical education in higher education: Three recommendations. *Quest*, **40**(1), 47-55.

LAWSON, H.A. (1979). Paths toward professionalization. *Quest*, **31**(2), 231-243.

LAWSON, H.A. (1980). Beyond teaching and ad hocracy: Increasing the sphere of influence and control for physical educationists. *Quest*, **32**, 22-30.

LAWSON, H.A. (1984). Problem setting for physical education and sport. *Quest*, **36**(1), 48-60.

LAWSON, H.A. (1985). Challenges to graduate education. *Journal of Physical Education, Recreation and Dance*, **56**(7), 23-25.

LAWSON, H.A. (1988). Physical education and the reform of undergraduate education. *Quest*, **40**(1), 12-32.

LAWSON, H.A., & Morford, W.R. (1979). The cross-disciplinary structure of kinesiology and sport studies: Distinctions, implications and advantages. *Quest*, **31**(2), 220-230.

LAWSON, H.A., & Sinclair, G.D. (1982). Generic and generalizable professional skills for the undergraduate major. *National Association for Physical Education in Higher Education Proceedings*, **3**, 107-114.

LOCKE, L.F., & Siedentop, D. (1980). Beyond arrogance and ad hominem: A reply to Hal Lawson. *Quest*, **32**(1), 31-43.

LOPIANO, D.A. (1984). How to pursue a sports management career. *Journal of Physical Education, Recreation and Dance*, **55**(8), 15-19.

LOUGHERY, T.J. (1985). Basic stuff in a professional preparation program. *Journal of Physical Education, Recreation and Dance*, **56**(8), 11-13.

LOUGHERY, T.J. (1987). Evaluating program effectiveness. *Journal of Physical Education, Recreation and Dance*, **58**(6), 63-65.

LUCAS, J.A. (1979). Sport history through biography. *Quest*, **31**(2), 216-221.

MAWSON, L.M. (1984). Insurance against the nation's risk: Extended professional preparation for physical education. *National Association for Physical Education in Higher Education Proceedings*, **5**, 138-145.

MAYNARD, J.A., & Leslie, D.R. (1988). Exercise science: An alternative major for the pre-health professions. *Journal of Physical Education, Recreation and Dance*, **59**(4), 65-67.

METHENY, E. (1967). *Movement and meaning*. New York: McGraw-Hill.

MILLER, D.M. (1987). Energizing the thinking dimensions of physical education. *Journal of Physical Education, Recreation and Dance*, **58**(8), 76-79.

OBERLE, G.H. (1988). A future direction plan for our professions. *Journal of Physical Education, Recreation and Dance*, **59**(1), 76-77.

O'BRIEN, D.B. (1985). A conversation between two frogs in the fog. *Journal of Physical Education, Recreation and Dance*, **56**(2), 54-55.

O'HANLON, J., & Wandzilak, T. (1980). Physical education: A professional field. *Quest*, **32**(1), 52-59.

OLIVER, B. (1988). Educational reform and physical education. *Journal of Physical Education, Recreation and Dance*, **59**(1), 68-71.

PARKHOUSE, B.L., & Ulrich, D.O. (1979). Sport management as a potential cross-discipline: A paradigm for theoretical development, scientific inquiry, and professional application. *Quest*, **31**(2), 264-276.

PARKS, J.B., & Quain, R.J. (1986). Curricular perspectives. *Journal of Physical Education, Recreation and Dance*, **57**(4), 22-26.

RAZOR, J.E. (1988). The Holmes Group proposal and implications for physical education as a "solid" subject matter (and other related problems). *Quest*, **40**(1), 33-46.

RIORDAN, J. (1979). Professional training in physical education in the U.S.S.R. *Quest*, **31**(1), 36-44.

ROBINSON, S.M. (1980). Anticipating the 1980s: Living and being in physical education. *Journal of Physical Education, Recreation and Dance*, **51**(8), 46-47.

ROSE, D.A. (1986). Is there a discipline of physical education? *Quest*, **38**(1), 1-21.

SAGE, G.H. (1984). The quest for identity in college physical education. *Quest*, **36**, 116-121.

SCAHILL, J.L. (1988). New P.E. career options—Time for assessment? *Journal of Physical Education, Recreation and Dance*, **59**(5), 65-67.

SCHWEBEL, M. (1985). The clash of cultures in academe: The university and the education faculty. *Journal of Teacher Education*, **36**(4), 2-7.

SCULLY, M.G. (1986, November 5). Study finds colleges torn by divisions, confused over roles. *The Chronicle of Higher Education*, pp. 1-9.

SHEEHAN, T. (1984). An alternative perspective of physical education in higher education. *National Association for Physical Education in Higher Education Proceedings*, **5**, 36-41.

SINGER, R.N. (1979). Future direction in the movement arts and sciences. *Quest*, **31**(2), 255-263.

STAFFORD, E. (1981). Changing trends in Wisconsin physical education. *Journal of Physical Education, Recreation and Dance*, **52**(9), 29-31.

STIER, W.F. (1986). Challenges facing physical education. Alternative career options. *Journal of Physical Education, Recreation and Dance*, **57**(8), 26-27.

TEMPLIN, T.J., Woodford, R., & Mulling, C. (1982). On becoming a physical educator: Occupational choice and the anticipatory socialization process. *Quest*, **34**(2), 119-133.

THOMAS, J.R. (1985). Physical education and paranoia—synonyms. *Journal of Physical Education, Recreation and Dance*, **56**(8), 20-22.

VANDERZWAAG, H.J. (1983). Coming out of the maze: Sport management, dance management, and exercise science—programs with a future. *Quest*, **35**(1), 66-73.

VINCENT, W.J., Winningham, S.N., & Caldwell, S.F. (1988). Department name change: A rationale for kinesiology. *Journal of Physical Education, Recreation and Dance*, **59**(7), 109-110.

WENDT, J. (1982). Coping skills: A goal of professional preparation. *National Association of Physical Education in Higher Education Proceedings*, **3**, 96-100.

WENDT, J. (1983). Professional preparation: A process of discovery. *Quest*, **35**(2), 182-189.

WILLIAMS, L.R.T. (1979). Undergraduate and graduate education in physical education in New Zealand over the next three decades. *Quest*, **31**(1), 71-76.

ZEIGLER, E.F. (1983). Relating a proposed taxonomy of sport and developmental physical activity to a planned inventory of scientific findings. *Quest*, **35**(1), 54-65.

Response to Franks' Paper

Frank I. Katch
University of Massachusetts

I am very pleased to offer a response to Franks' paper. This gives me a chance to be reflective on a topic about which I feel strongly, and allows me the liberty of trying to make the case that Franks' paper did not go far enough.

Franks played the role of the consummate politician. He was careful to bless many who have made significant contributions to our field, but he was also careful not to step on any toes. He skillfully tiptoed through the tulips, didn't ruffle any of the budding daffodils and, to my way of thinking, has suggested we fill up with 80 octane gasoline in an Edsel automobile. It would have been more useful if he had concluded with a plan of action for a structure for an undergraduate kinesiology program rather than simply to report about the current state of affairs. Such information is surely helpful in some ways but it doesn't address the salient issue.

The prior history of our field has shown that we are great talkers, that we love surveys, and that we revel in all types of planning maneuvers. But I believe more should and could be done, and in a faster time frame. Franks proposes a 5-year plan that he hopes will result in a consensus. He also doesn't believe that arriving at common names and definitions is an important issue for our field. I disagree. It is important to come to grips squarely with such issues, and the sooner the better. There's little point in beating around the bush much longer. It's certainly not a matter for discussion ad nauseam (25-30 years is surely long enough!). Franks believes it is beyond the point at which a leader in the field can provide the basis for a consensus, or a particular school can decide what it has done so that school's program can become the model.

To those who would change the current name of their department, please don't fall into the trap of simply repackaging your curricular efforts with a coat of white paint so that the new label shines brightly when viewed with rose colored glasses. The new name shouldn't pretend that things are truly different if in fact they are not. A newly named department that doesn't alter its basic administrative structure and focus has indulged in nothing more than name changing for its own sake. I would submit that phys ed by any other name would still be phys ed!

One can appreciate the need for faculty groups to continually seek to redefine their own identity, and to periodically cleanse their house to get it in order. And I admit that's a difficult, evolving process. If the stated missions and objectives of a particular unit are primarily teacher training, there is little need to change the name of the degree program from physical education to some other name such as kinesiology. It would seem to make more sense to offer an undergraduate degree in Preparation of Gym Teachers than to disguise the title with white paint in hopes of achieving greater respectability.

Adhering to what Franks recommends would in fact probably produce a smorgasbord curriculum of a little of this, a little of that, all sprinkled with good intentions and good will. After all, we are a tolerant group. AAHPER became AAHPERD, and more councils were created so that more interests could be represented. AAHPERD has constructed a large tent and its top covers a broad area. Currently 117 different names are used to describe our field of study! The titles include health, dance, recreation, teaching, safety, fitness, administration, coaching, athletics, and sports management, and the list continues to cycle through many permutations and combinations.

If we wait for a consensus, what is likely to happen? Does Franks really believe national debate can do other than create a goulash of proposals? A little of this, a little of that, all sprinkled with good intentions and good will. A consensus of currently accepted practices does not result in a true validation of such practices. I would argue that current (and popular) choices should not serve as the sole basis for establishing the core subject matter content of our field. Not only is there likely to be no consensus in 5 years—25 years would not be long enough!

I would also argue mildly against Franks' thesis that the 5th year should be devoted to professional preparation. What I take Franks to mean is that student teachers should be prepared in content oriented courses in 4 years, as in a kinesiology core program, and then left to finish a 5th year to learn all they can about the teaching process. Locke has just made the persuasive argument that this can't be done. He believes there's simply too much to teach, and a 5th year just won't work. I could agree with Locke, but I believe a workable model would separate two major parts of what is now predominantly "physical education" in the colleges and universities. I would opt for a core as the academic discipline and would hope that the teaching function would be allowed to flourish independently with its own curricula and programs. The California model is sound; the "how to" of the pedagogical domain should survive without intrusion under the umbrella of the academic discipline.

It is important to keep in mind that students who currently elect to major in physical education don't all opt to pursue teaching per se as their career. To infiltrate the core of the academic discipline with required "how to" courses is a throwback to the good old days when the title "gym teacher" was in fact an appropriate description of what most phys ed majors did as their primary responsibility. It is estimated that as many as one half or more of the majors in physical education do not become teachers!

Figure 1 shows a 15-year-old model for a proposed academic field of study called exercise science (the name could easily have been kinesiology). The model was developed in secret. The president of the City University of New York asked John Magel, then the department chair of Queens College, to develop a workable plan to help solve the budget crisis in higher education at the City University of New York. John asked me to help develop the plan, and so I did. Locke says there were disciples of Berkeley running around doing such things in the 1960s and '70s—and yes, I was one of them—and it was with energy and conviction

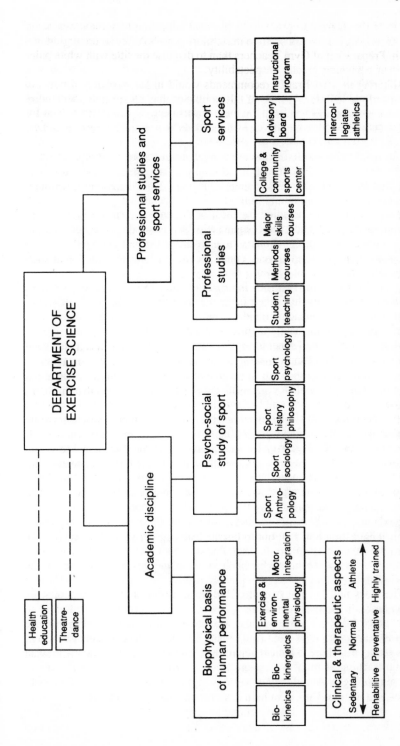

Figure 1 — The inclusion of professional studies and sport services within a department of exercise science.

that we began to create our blueprint. In this model, teacher preparation was neatly tucked away into its own package under a department of professional studies and sports services. The intention was to clearly separate the subject matter core we called the academic discipline from the traditional programs that included student teaching, methods courses, and skills courses for majors. If push had come to shove, we would have been perfectly content to separate the professional studies and sport sciences programs from the main department. This was envisioned for health education and theater–dance. The dashed lines in Figure 1 indicate releasing these programs to function on their own.

Our major goal was to integrate the biophysical and psychosocial subareas of study within a single department. It just didn't make sense to us then, nor does it now, that each college in the system (Queens, Brooklyn, Hunter, Lehman, Baruch, City, and the Community Colleges) should operate a department of health and physical education, including for most of the units, departments of dance, recreation, intramurals, and intercollegiate athletics. It certainly was not economical, nor would it have been visionary, to expect that the glut of physical education teachers graduating each year could secure teaching jobs in the already overcrowded public school system.

It was not surprising that such internal pressures forced many departments in North America to reevaluate their curricular objectives. After all, "old time" physical education was changing rapidly. The elitists, as Locke named them, were restless about the pressing need for change, and rightly so. It wasn't the discipline based ideas that were out of sync; it was the traditionalists or so-called pedagogical experts who failed the disciplinarians. Where was the body of knowledge about the teaching process? Who were the educational theorists who produced new knowledge about motor skill development and acquisition, optimal learning strategies, theories of play, and so on? I'm sure it was not in the colleges of education where the traditional physical education programs were held in low esteem by administrators and others who were hoping to see real progress made in our field.

And so it is you, the Larry Lockes of our field, who must shoulder much of the blame for what you have created. The focus of physical education has changed dramatically, even in the last 10 years. There is today a greater need than ever to redirect our energies to make the academic discipline approach even stronger and more widespread. Franks' proposal is a "modernized" throwback to the good old days. It's wishey-washey. A department of kinesiology (or exercise science), where the focus is on the academic discipline approach, should seek an amicable divorce from the teacher preparation specialists whose primary mission is to prepare teachers who teach exercise and physical activities in the schools.

This does not, by any stretch of the imagination, imply there should be isolation between the two approaches. To the contrary, cross-fertilization is an essential process that will enhance those who are discipline based and those whose mission is service oriented and professional. I believe that both constructs will become stronger if there is a clear separation of function. Individuals who wish to pursue teaching as their profession need to learn everything they can about the teaching process. And if they must become proficient in a myriad of physical activities so they can "do it" in the classroom, then so be it.

In this context, Locke has stated that research about the teaching process has been, over the past 15 years, the fastest growing segment of the research enterprise in the physical education domain. He certainly is entitled to his opinion, but I question the validity of such a claim. Perhaps Locke and *his* loyal band of disciples should hire a savvy PR firm so more of us can become enlightened about such momentous accomplishments. As a "disciplinarian elitist" might respond, "Where's the beef"?

In conclusion, I do apologize somewhat for commenting about Locke's various incantations, but I really couldn't resist. If Franks had known Locke's essay would have contained such acid insights, he may have chosen to reconsider some of his position statements. But as my younger son says, "Dad, that's history."

Summary

First, Franks' paper, while useful for enlightening us about the current status of the coursework in our field, didn't deliver enough. I don't think a consensus will work, and the time frames are off. I don't think physical education can be all things to all people. It's time for a change. I'm also leery that a 5th-year program can really solve the problems related to effective teaching. That's something for the teacher training specialists to work out.

Second, I believe strongly that we should approach the topic under discussion with a sense of tolerance and respect. This is a time for change, not a time for war. It may be, however, that when the dialogue gets down to brass tacks between the disciplinarians and the "pedagogical kinesiologists," a lot of toes will be stepped on, many feathers will be ruffled, and it may cause a lot of winds to blow, and otherwise.

I would propose, with the enthusiasm of a Berkeley graduate (but not as an elitist), that we go forward to create a valid model for our field of study so we will be ready for the 21st century. I endorse the concept of kinesiology as the common name for the subject field of study. And I make the distinction that the professional studies courses (methods, skills, student teaching, and so forth), should *not* be part of the kinesiology major. Those interested in becoming gym teachers in the schools should do so because it is a perfectly respectable and admirable profession that requires no excuses from anyone. For the new graduates of the newly named discipline, however, the choice will now be theirs.

Goodbye "Physical Education," Hello "Exercise and Sport Science"

Richard C. Nelson
Pennsylvania State University

The question being asked is, Should the name of the undergraduate major, physical education, be changed? Under the assumption that the modern curriculum is designed to prepare future professionals in a variety of fields in addition to preparing them for teaching, then my answer to that question is a resounding, unequivocal yes. There is ample evidence that the expression *physical education* is commonly understood to mean the teaching of motor skills in the schools and is incapable of embracing the fields of exercise, sport, physical activity, and many others. This is true in spite of the efforts and hopes of many of us who have been in physical education for many years.

The Colorado/Texas Dilemma

Perhaps the best way to bring one aspect of this question into clear focus is to examine what has happened in the states of Colorado and Texas in recent years. In response to the national concern for quality education, emphasis has shifted from education courses to the basic disciplines. In these two states it is no longer possible to major in any field of education at the undergraduate level. This means that students can no longer major in such fields as art education, science education, mathematics education, music education, industrial arts education, or physical education. They must first earn a bachelor's degree in their discipline and then take pedagogical courses in order to be certified to teach. This means that the students must major in art, science, mathematics, music, and "physical." Yes, physical! What constitutes the curriculum in a major called physical? This scenario demonstrates clearly that the name *physical education* can no longer be a viable title for an undergraduate major even if the curriculum is limited to teacher preparation. To suggest the use of this term to describe a modern curriculum with multiple career options is, in my opinion, absolutely ludicrous and clearly impossible to defend.

The Nelson "National Survey"

In an attempt to shed some light on this question, I decided to conduct an informal, nonscientific survey (pilot study) to assess the perceptions of a sample

58

of people regarding the following three terms: physical education, kinesiology, and exercise and sport science. Respondents were asked to describe briefly what comes to mind when hearing each term, or were asked, "If I told you I was a physical educator (kinesiologist, or exercise and sport scientist) what do you think I would do in my work?" Colleagues at Arizona State Univesity (Charles Corbin and Phil Martin), University of Iowa (Jim Hay), and University of Wisconsin (Bill Morgan) assisted with the data collection. A total of 75 responses came from these groups. The majority of responses were obtained at Penn State with a few being recorded while I was traveling. The number of replies for each term was slightly different: PE—209, kinesiology—184, and exercise and sport science—210. Furthermore, no attempt was made to determine the age, background, gender, and so forth, of the respondents. In spite of the obvious flaws in experimental design and sampling procedures, the results may still be of importance. If nothing else, they will provide the only data collected to date on this subject, create the basis for discussion, and hopefully stimulate enough interest for the Academy or some other organization to conduct a bona fide, national survey.

After the data were collected it was necessary to categorize the responses. Because of the open-ended nature of the survey, a wide variety of terms were obtained. In some cases arbitrary decisions had to be made in creating logical groupings of responses. In order to eliminate any bias on the part of the author, the data were tabulated by a doctoral student in biomechanics from India whose previous undergraduate and master's degree work was in mechanical engineering. The results of this data analysis are presented in Table 1.

Table 1

Distribution of Responses in Percentages

| | Term | | |
Responses	Physical education ($n = 209$)	Kinesiology ($n = 184$)	Exercise & sport science ($n = 210$)
Don't know	0.0	37.5	5.2
Movement science	0.5	35.1	4.5
Fitness	16.3	0.2	13.5
Gym class	79.7	2.2	13.8
Athletic training/physical therapy	0.7	1.5	12.6
Research	0.5	0.5	16.3
Physiology/anatomy	0.0	7.3	8.7
Science	0.0	4.6	8.5
Academia (study of)	0.0	3.2	6.9
Medicine	0.0	1.4	2.0
Miscellaneous	2.3	6.5	8.0

The data for *physical education* show very cearly the perception that this term refers to gym classes (79.7%) and fitness (16.3%). These results are so overwhelming that it should dispel any doubts that physical education as a term cannot, and will not, reflect any activity beyond gym class teaching. It should be noted that not one respondent fell in the "Don't know" category. The results for *kinesiology* are also very clear as 37.5% of the respondents indicated they didn't know what it meant, whereas 35% gave movement science or its equivalent as their answer. The only other category with over 5% responses was "physiology/anatomy," which received 7.3%. These results indicate that kinesiology is a relatively unknown term and one that conveys a broad, nonspecific description.

The third term, *exercise and sport science*, elicited by far the most inclusive and interesting responses. The variety of responses was clearly evident as 10 categories received responses from 2% to 16.3%. Four categories received over 10%: fitness, gym class, athletic training/physical therapy, and research. The wide range of responses indicates that this title provides an umbrella that includes many of the activities involving human movement, health, exercise, sports, and research. If the purpose of the undergraduate major is to provide academic preparation for a variety of careers, then *exercise and sport science* clearly represents a good choice.

Summary

The Texas/Colorado dilemma shows clearly how vulnerable a profession named physical education can be in light of the current status of education in the U.S. To suggest that this field is based on an academic subject matter called "physical" is absolutely absurd. Such a revelation creates an embarrassment for our field while providing amusement for persons in other fields. The Nelson National Survey revealed the following facts regarding the perception of the three terms surveyed: (a) *physical education* = gym class, fitness, (b) *kinesiology* = "?", movement science, physiology, and (c) *exercise and sport science* = research, athletic training or physical therapy, fitness, science, physiology, and academia.

Conclusion

If the purpose of the undergraduate major is to educate and prepare gym class teachers, then physical education is the ideal name. However, if the purpose is to educate and prepare students for a variety of careers, then exercise and sport science is my recommendation for the name of the undergraduate major, and we can confidently say, "Goodbye physical education."

Unsolicited Comment on the Name of the Academy

The results of the Nelson National Survey and the consequences of the restructuring of the Alliance that occurred a few years ago have led me to consider the appropriateness of the name, American Academy of Physical Education. Under the Alliance structure, the National Association for Sport and Physical Education (NASPE) consists of nine academies: curriculum and instruction, history, philosophy, motor development, sport psychology, exercise physiology, kinesiology, sociology, and sport art. Unfortunately, the use of the term *academy* creates considerable confusion regarding the American Academy of Physical Education. No doubt many young professionals in the field assume that AAPE is just another "academy." In light of the survey results it would appear that the AAPE could logically be perceived to be the "American Academy of Gym Class Teachers." If that is the case, then many of the other academies would appear to be more meaningful, interesting, and important to young professionals than an academy composed of gym teachers. Such a situation greatly diminishes the honor and prestige of being elected to membership in our Academy, especially if it assumed anyone can belong merely by signing up and paying the dues. As a consequence, it is my recommendation that serious consideration be given to changing the name of the AAPE to one of the following: American (Academy, Institute, Society, or College) of Exercise and Sport Science.

Acknowledgment

The author wishes to thank Somadeepti Chengalur, PhD student in biomechanics, for her assistance in the data analysis and slide preparation.

Changing the Name Has its Problems

Celeste Ulrich
University of Oregon

According to the reports of social psychologists, the changing of one's name may produce an awesome problem of social identity. Even if the change is actively sought by the individual, the actual fait accompli causes identity mutations that insist upon adaptation. However, it is noted that with social approval and endorsement, the change may lead to a status change that brings with it selected advantages and disadvantages.

For empirical confirmation, one need only note the traditional and socially accepted expectation that a woman assume her husband's last name when entering into marriage. For years, such a name change was considered a social asset, and I can easily believe that some of the women within the Academy must have experimented, as I did, by joining your name with the family name of your current beau just to see "what it looked like." It has not been until relatively recently that women have reported some unease with that tradition, suggesting the disadvantages outweighed the advantages, and they have encouraged society to construct the social paradigm that allows women to keep their own name after marriage or to hyphenate their family name with that of their husband, or, in some rare instances, to acknowledge that it might be acceptable for the husband to assume the wife's family name.

For those individuals who have desired to change their name in less traditional operations, the public record agencies and the courts have permitted a person to do so, albeit with a plethora of red tape. There are a myriad of reasons for name changing. Some individuals wish to discard their established identity and start anew; others seek to facilitate the pronunciation of their name; others dislike the connotation of their name; still others seek a new name to better explain themselves. There may be reason to believe that professional and disciplinary areas are not too different from individuals and, at some point in their history, for numerous reasons, come to believe that a name change will facilitate their function or will better describe their mission.

Physical education has been considering a name change for well over two decades. The driving desire to better identify the field of endeavor has been cited usually as the reason but, in addition, there have been covert reasons reflecting concerns about name connotations, academic respectability, and a new image. At least three national committees have explored the possibility of name change.

Some of the resultant reports have suggested attention to sport, some have emphasized performance science, and still others have stressed human movement.

Attention to the subject matter suggested has been cited as the primary need, and various emphases have been subsumed under the aegis of some already identified names (most notably kinesiology). Some committees have suggested the addition or substitution of words employed in the study of the concerns that make up physical education (human ecology, sport science, human performance and development) or have even coined new words (usually of a Greek or Latin base) to add to the academic vocabulary. Not one of the reports has ever been accorded the blessing of any major professional organization, although college and university departments have adopted some of the suggestions and incorporated the ideas into a new name to be included in their institutional vocabulary. For the most part, we have continued to plod along with the appellation physical education, feeling increasingly uncomfortable with the limitations that name imposes, yet fearing to abandon the security of recognition afforded by the name and a bit reluctant to engage in anticipated battles to once again prove ourselves and earn an established niche in the academic community.

This lack of general consensus guarantees that we will continue to address the subject of name change in meetings such as this one and perpetuate our concerns without coming to closure. My own guess is that an eventual name change will not be legislated or adopted but, rather like Topsy, will just grow upon us. As more and more departments of physical education in colleges and universities undertake name changes; when those changes ripple into the public schools, then, and only then, will there be an organized effort on the part of AAHPERD and NASPE to orchestrate the profession's commitment to a different appellation.

Part of the difficulty in effecting a name change has always been in attempting to identify what it is that physical education is about. To the majority of nonphysical educators, physical education is a "do-good" activity that claims to improve human fitness through physical activity and utilizes skills in structured performance such as sport, aquatics, gymnastics, and dance as modalities to achieve its mission.

To the professional physical educator, physical education is most often understood in the classic description offered by J.F. Williams as "the sum total of human activity, selected as to kind and structured as to outcome" with emphases on the behavioral and biological concomitants. At best, it is a vague description suggesting that anything which sponsors motoric interaction with the individual's environment is within the province of physical education.

Actually, the majority of pedagogy concerned with physical education is based on skill acquisition. The motor skills acquired are used to promulgate an elusive and obtuse condition identified as "fitness" and are often coordinated with play behavior. Thus, play, fitness, and movement become identifiable concepts that are essential to physical education and somehow should be implied in any name change that is proposed. It becomes obvious that finding the proper words to incorporate such concepts is difficult, so we have taken to stringing words together or have depended upon a word that has had limited and convoluted acceptance in the language or has been newly coined.

Several things can happen when a name change is made, even if the mutation has been endorsed by the professionals involved in the area. First, it is necessary to find some general consistency of understanding. If the term human ecology means one thing to a group of biologists, another to psychologists, and yet another to engineers, the difficulty of gaining consensus is intensified.

As selected states have insisted that professional education have a subject matter field (i.e., music education utilizes music, business education utilizes business, etc.), many physical educators, understanding that "physical" is not a recognizable subject matter field, have turned to the word *kinesiology* as a tag. They believe that it has the advantage of being known in academia and of being identified with the study of human movement as promoted by physical educators. However, opponents of such a name change suggest that the Greek root connotation of the word *kinesiology* conveys a kinetic interpretation that has scientific overtones in the area of the natural sciences and that seems to abrogate responsibility for sociopsychological behavioral consequences.

The names *sport sciences* and *human performance* suggest a limited insight (in the case of sport sciences) or a catholic concern that may be too broad to offer reasonable limitations (in the case of human performance). For example, sport sciences suggests a specific method of investigation into very selected activities whereas human performance offers no perimeters for definition and ignores physical educators' traditional concern for the human play behaviors. Both names are inattentive to the acknowledged pedagogical emphases in physical education and might ignore by omission the subscription to fitness.

Some physical educators, such as our colleague Earle Zeigler, have continually implored us to adhere to the European tradition by including the term sport as part of our identification. Such an admonition should not be ignored but should not be adopted without a great deal of thought. Fortunately or unfortunately, in the United States the term sport carries with it the organizational inference of "athletics," thus relating physical educators to athletes, coaches, and athletic administrators. The organization of athletics as a special form of sport is so confused in the North American culture that I believe there is a real danger in attempting to intertwine a disciplinary interest with the professional format of an operation that harbors both confusion and distrust. Just as biology had to divest itself of medicine, so, I believe, we must divest ourselves of the responsibility for athletics. It will remain proper and fitting for those who wish to enter the area of athletic organization and administration to do so through the field of what is presently called physical education. They may also gain entry through the fields of business, behavioral science, public relations, and communications. There will continue to be selected situations in which it will be necessary for athletics to share facilities, equipment, and even personnel with physical education, but such sharing should be mandated by expedience rather than design.

Of special importance in changing one's name is the responsibility of having that name change acceptable to those who will employ it. Many of our colleagues have seen the attempt at name changing to be an exercise in futility for purposes not necessary. The question of academic respectability is often addressed derisively, with inferences being made that it would be more desirable to improve our operation and gain respectability than attempt to snag it with a name change. Others have believed that any name change suggests a newness that in these days of program cutting would bode poorly for physical education's future.

They point out some of the problems encountered by those departments (which they eagerly identify) that adopted a new name and were consequently seen as the new kid on the block and, as a result, "last to come, first to go." They suggest further that our staid professionals do not readily associate with change and consequently feel uncomfortable and disloyal to any new name. Administrators have a penchant to translate this discomfort as infidelity to the area of concern. With no loyal supporters, the area accedes to elimination.

But so far we have addressed all of the difficulties of name change and some of the liabilities. It should be acknowledged that there appear to be selected benefits and opportunities. Assuming that the name changers are committed to the new name and have gained the support of those in the central administration who can influence its acceptance, there are some assets that can be anticipated.

For a long time, physical education has been identified with health education, dance, athletics, and recreation, and the lines between those individual areas have been so blurred as to defy identification. The assumption of a new name helps to clarify the exact subject matter area of physical education, giving each of the other areas a more definitive claim as to their responsibilities. By virtue of its newness, a name change divests all of the areas of the traditional baggage of historic association. This permits and encourages new opportunities for interaction and certainly has the tendency to reduce the paranoia of health educators, recreators, athletic administrators, coaches, and dance educators regarding their relationship with physical education's "big daddy" image.

Moreover, a name change signals to the educational establishment as a whole that physical education is undergoing a metamorphosis and must be reexamined in light of its enlightened concerns for human development and welfare. In addition, the foundations and governmental departments and bureaus that control contract research and investigatory grants seemingly have been favorably impressed with name changes for physical education. They seem more disposed to consider proposals in light of their implications and merit than in respect to preconceived ideas regarding the identity of physical educators and the implied limitations of scholarship that have been vested in the athletic-related image.

The name change also has the potential to help identify the administrative unit with which physical educators can be most comfortably housed. Although different institutions have different patterns of identification, it seems increasingly apparent that physical educators should not be automatically housed in departments and schools of education, nor should they be automatically amalgamated into departments of biology, sociology, and psychology in schools of arts and sciences, or in colleges and departments of home economics and engineering. The name changes that have occurred have promoted the idea that a division for the study of human performance is an enlightened and realistic path to future organization in education and that such organization accommodates well the area practiced by physical educators.

Name changes do not operate as a magic potion, however. Although they insist upon acceptance and commitment, such reactions are more carefully nourished by time and use rather than by edict and announcement. The problems incurred by name changes are not always simple ones and are often made more complex by the absence of unanimity on the part of all of us who are practitioners.

It has been interesting to watch the area of concern that I knew as social work (contained within departments of sociology in most institutions of higher education) emerge as units of human services, independent of sociology by the choice of both social workers and their parent creators, the sociologists. They are certainly in the midst of a struggle, but it appears that human services is establishing itself on many fronts and will, within the next decade, assume its position among the discretely identifiable areas of professional concern.

Physical education, in its attempt to find its disciplinary concerns and its professional responsibilities, has a difficult task. It is a task that has its problems, but it also has implied rewards in both the exercise and the result. I truly believe that we are up to it.

Don't Forget the Profession
When Choosing a Name!

Earle F. Zeigler
The University of Western Ontario

My objective in this paper is first to convince you, the members of the American Academy of Physical Education, that you should be playing an active, key role in helping our field to decide upon an appropriate name by which to call itself. Second, I wish to urge you to remember that we are striving for professional status, and that this should be reflected in any name that is recommended for the field.

Whoever first said it is a crazy world—the manager of the first overcrowded lunatic asylum, I guess—knew what he was talking about! Here I am close to the end of 50 years in the field of physical education, and my first doctoral student in the area of sport and physical education philosophy has recently published an article arguing that physical education should be abolished. (I really convinced him, didn't I?) In fact, before that he went so far as to approach the education committee of his state legislature to request the abandonment of physical education classes and the substitution of classes taught by capable sport skills instructors instead.

However, what VanderZwaag concluded most recently was that "Physical educators are beyond the point of danger"; they are "lost in the shuffle, and have been for some time" (1983, p. 67). What VanderZwaag proposes is a major reorganization so that the field would no longer exist as such—it would become instead (a) sport management, (b) dance management, and (c) exercise science. He argues that such a change is needed because this would truly inform a typically ignorant public about what it is that we do (p. 73). From this point on, then, I presume I am speaking to you as a sport manager!

An Endless Search for Identity

Seriously, this argument does give one pause for thought. As an incipient profession, we have for far too long been searching for an identity. Such a search obviously has a close relationship to what we call ourselves. We, as members of the Academy, are all old enough to remember when pressure came in the early 1960s for our profession to go all out to promote a substantive disciplinary emphasis. Believe it or not, it was actually a generation ago when Conant attacked our field so directly and destructively. C.H. McCloy had warned us in the late 1950s (about the time when Sputnik went up) that we had better improve our scholarly efforts. His warnings from within the field were heard but not really assimilated. However, after the "infamous charge" made against us by Conant in 1963, the fat was in the fire.

This was the period, then, when Arthur Esslinger (1966), Franklin Henry (1964), and others sought to rally our forces with a solid response to the challenge from a respected university educator—a former president of dear old Harvard University—who had taken unto himself the prerogative of assessing the status of U.S. education. Conant's attack was followed shortly thereafter (in the Midwest, for example) by the efforts of Art Daniels (1965) and King McCristal (Zeigler & McCristal, 1967) to get the Big Ten Body-of-Knowledge Project going. Many of us in the Academy and our colleagues in our home institutions were involved, also, in the effort to define a discipline, including whether physical education could somehow qualify under such a rubric. In the process we heard about such theoretical constructs as multidisciplines, cross-disciplines, and interdisciplines. In fact, I offered as an explanation of the progressive experience our field was undergoing (Zeigler, 1972) that we were moving from a multidiscipline to a cross-discipline to an interdiscipline. I actually published several articles enlightening the masses about this significant transition (see Figure 1).

This sounded great until, a few years later, a bright young professional from Georgia Tech took me aside and politely inquired whether the actual direction of the disciplinary movement I postulated wasn't exactly the opposite. The only response I could think of at the moment was that what I was describing would eventually take place—but over a longer period of time. However, at this very moment, I regret to inform you that I still see no noticeable movement in the direction I had predicted originally. The predicted centripetal movement of the various subdisciplinary aspects of our field toward a central core does not seem to be occurring. The centrifugal breakaway movement of the field's knowledge segments has continued on unabated (see Figure 2)!

So what has been happening? Basically, there has been a frantic scramble by a great many people to get on *some* disciplinary bandwagon. This might not be so bad, except that in the process many of these same people have practically deserted their own field of physical education—the subject matter in which the overwhelming majority have received their highest degree. Are these people saying that VanderZwaag is right? What really troubles me is that, in the process of the "respectability scramble," we in the Academy have been muddling along in our own inimitable way, evidently not willing to take the time to discover our own purpose and our true identity. We are too busy fussing around with our individual trees (or subdisciplines) to worry about the future of our own forest, in which we are literally struggling for survival! Out there "in the larger forest," by the way, one hardly knows what a discipline is anymore, and we really don't know either to what extent our field deserves such a designation. The result is that many of us are disavowing our own field or profession and seeking some sort of status (often marginal and dubious) with a discipline of longer standing.

What does all this boil down to? I believe that what is emerging is that in one regard we are quite similar to the professions of law, medicine, and engineering. By this I mean that we are quasi-professional and quasi-disciplinary. These other professional schools are well established, of course, but during their earlier

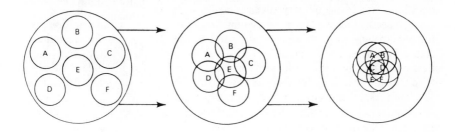

MULTIDISCIPLINE ⟶ CROSSDISCIPLINE ⟶ INTERDISCIPLINE

Key:

A = Physiologic

B = Sociologic

C = Psychologic

D = Biomechanic

E = Historical, Philosophic, Comparative

F = Others?

Figure 1 — Physical education—a multidiscipline on the way toward becoming a cross-discipline?

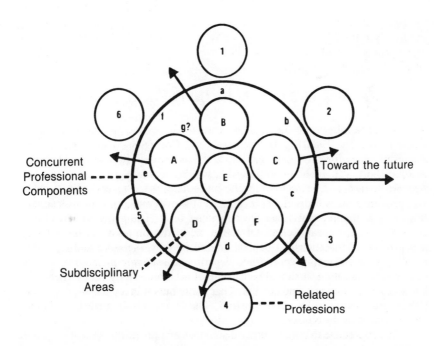

Figure 2 — Physical education—the profession from 1970 to 1990.

development they found it necessary to bring in people from other disciplines to help them. Talking to business administration professors, I find that many of them are even today unsure of their status as an emerging profession, and the question of their disciplinary status is really wide open.

It seems that we are in a situation similar to business administration. We too are striving for professional status, and we are also striving for disciplinary status. Where we are different from business, however, is that they have a great desire to retain their ties with businessmen in the public sector, while at the same time they are searching for ways to raise their status in the academic firmament. We, conversely, seem to wish to deliberately distance ourselves from the professional physical and health education practitioners—and especially from a breed known as coaches—people who are pursuing their duties and responsibilities for better or worse out in the communities. Second, to raise our status in academic circles, we are assuming the coloration of the other disciplines instead of literally reaching out to bring them in with us by offering them greater than 50% appointments.

Now, to make things even worse, because of the recommendations of the infamous Holmes Group Report (1986), legislators in various regions are telling universities that the names of any university academic programs shall not have the word *education* in them. And we all know where that leaves physical education, a program that has typically been placed under, or has almost grown up under, divisions, schools, or colleges of education. Thus the scramble is on to devise some sort of descriptive and/or esoteric name that will describe physical education in such a way that (a) any identification with a school of education will be obliterated, and (b) other departments on campus will immediately think that something new, mysterious, and truly of a scholarly nature is going on in a building commonly referred to as a "temple of sweat." I guess you can imagine what my unprintable reaction is to this deliberate attempt to eradicate our heritage in an effort to gain a spurious level of academic respectability.

Recommended Criteria for the Elusive Appellation

You are all familiar with the present thrust to find respectability by assuming a new name. The 1988 Big Ten conference in Chicago struggled with criteria and terminology for 2-1/2 days and settled the matter definitively. The new name is to be short; yet, it should define what we do, what we study, what we are, what we are not, and be *the* label for the entire field, not just a part of it. It should also provide a basis for political leverage and should enhance campus standing. But, wait a minute, that's just the beginning of it. The name should also be accurate, valid, relevant, clear, attractive, help with professional sponsorship, and provide connotation and denotation and be both inclusive and exclusive. Finally, after enhancing appropriate department academic location relative to higher administration, it should be capable of accommodating future changes in knowledge, technology, and careers. That really puts it in a nutshell, doesn't it? (With appreciation to Dr. Bob Morford, The University of British Columbia, who attended as an observer.)

We appreciate that many other disciplines and professions seem to be able to divide and subdivide and still (somehow) call themselves by one name (e.g., anthropology, medicine), but somehow the field of physical education can't boast of a similar achievement. If we care to adorn ourselves with such names as human kinetics, ergonomics, exercise science, sport studies, anthropokineticology, kinesiology, and so on, no euphemism is going to protect us if we aren't doing the job in the field that is needed! (As Shakespeare stated in *Romeo and Juliet*, "What's in a name? That which we call a rose by any other name would smell as sweet.")

Reasons Why the Name *Physical Education* Should Be Dropped!

Should the name *physical education* be dropped? Even disregarding (a) what VanderZwaag has said, (b) how the disciplinary emphasis has affected us in this transitional period of the 1980s leading toward that mythical year 2001, and (c) the castigation we have (almost accidentally) received as fallout from the Holmes Report—on my own and despite my great loyalty to my adopted profession—I have concluded somewhat sadly that the name *physical education* as our only title has outlived its usefulness and should be phased out at the university level at least. How this could or should be handled at the high-school, middle-school, or elementary-school level is another matter that will be discussed shortly. Calling us something else in out-of-school situations should be no problem, because our adult clients out there in public, private, and commercial agencies most certainly don't want to think they are still taking part in physical education, the dreaded "PE" of their school years.

There are several good reasons for my opinion on this delicate subject. First, there is an opprobrium about the term *physical education* that we just can't seem to erase, and, frankly, many of the younger members of our profession are literally ashamed of it. Second, it does indeed imply a mind–body dichotomy that has been exploded theoretically—no matter how carefully we try to explain the concept of education *through* the medium of the physical. Third, people invariably associate the term *physical education* with something that happens in the schools only and not on a lifelong basis. Unfortunately, many people hated it during their schooldays, and they don't want to continue with it in their leisure when their formal education is over.

Fourth, and I regret the necessity of making such a seemingly destructive statement (especially since I hold a doctorate in education), the term *physical education* perpetuates our identity with the professional education enterprise that is unfortunately regarded as "the lowest of the low" on just about every campus I have ever visited. Fifth, and finally, in highly competitive sport or athletics (a term used primarily in North America), administrators and coaches have their own problems, especially in those universities where extensive commercialization of intercollegiate sport has caused athletics and physical education to sever almost all relationships. Athletics seems quite happy not to have physical education in its midst unless, of course, having it there brings supportive revenue (e.g., percentages of coaches' salaries being paid in this way).

The Perpetuation of a Blurred Image

Despite all of the changes that have occurred in the past 25 years, we would be hard pressed to deny that our profession has perpetuated such a blurred image that the public and even our own professional practitioners have been confused about our long-range aims and specific yearly objectives. This confusion has often been unconsciously transmitted to professional students, who find themselves at a loss when faced with a need to explain to parents and the general public what our field can and should do, both with children and young people, in the recommended daily programs in schools and universities. This confusion is even more evident as we seek to expand our territory by promoting a "womb to tomb" responsibility to work with the accelerated, the normal, and the special populations of all ages within our society.

As difficult as it may be, I believe that our profession should come to grips with the issue right now that the average physical education graduate is still typically a "jack-of-all-trades and master of none"! This is what *we* have been, and this is what they presently are. Can we possibly argue that this is a good thing, or is it bad and should it be changed? I firmly believe it should be changed. After many years I have come to believe that the profession has a duty and responsibility to work its way through to an appropriate name and a consensual taxonomy of knowledge for our work, on this continent at least. Every self-respecting profession has a body of knowledge. What is ours? Where is it? We should be able to look forward to a day in the not-too-distant future when we would have our theory and tenable hypotheses steadily growing and arranged as principles for daily use by our professional practitioners (see Figure 3).

Confused Terminology Has Got Us Stumped!

All of these names for the field that have been bandied about have brought us to a state of mass confusion. The term *sport and physical education* is now recommended by NASPE within the Alliance to describe *the professional entity* in the United States. In Canada it is still *physical and health education* in the schools. However, the terms *physical education and sport* and *sport* are now more popular in other countries that identify with the Western world and the European continent, respectively. In my opinion, no one of these names, or combination of names, is going to make it in the long run.

Agreement about a name, a taxonomy for our subject matter, and the steady development of a undergirding body of knowledge would reasonably soon place our field in a position in which a professional practitioner would be recognized as a such-and-such no matter what position that person held within the field—or for that matter in which state or territory such professional service was carried out. Reaching consensus at this late date will undoubtedly be extremely difficult; however, it is now essential that we strive for such an objective. Further, I believe that the Academy should take the lead in this urgent matter.

Therefore, in my opinion, the time is overdue for us to bring our field's image into sharper focus for the sake of our colleagues and students, not to mention the public at large. I must as well climb right out on a limb about what it is for which we should be responsible. We could call ourselves *human motor performance*, but this may not sound sufficiently academic for some. *Movement arts and science* has possibilities. The term *kinesiology* has been in the dictionary for decades, but we would have to broaden the definition that is there. What we are fundamentally involved with is "developmental physical activity in sport,

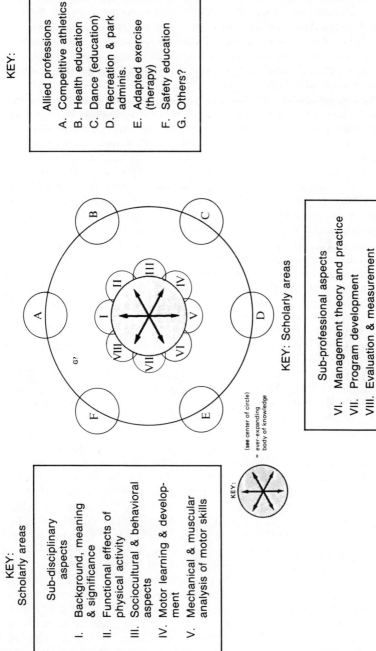

Figure 3 — Schema for the profession's developing body of knowledge.

exercise, and related expressive movement''—and that's it! The late Elizabeth Halsey recommended it long ago, but the time was not yet ripe for its acceptance.

Quite simply, our profession should be promoting such developmental physical activity for people of all ages. Further, we in the Academy should be "professing" our theoretical and applied knowledge to help our practitioners in the field. The time is past due to make our body of knowledge available through computer technology in a variety of ways (e.g., ordered principles, expert systems). In the process we must also convey to the public that we are not typically qualified to be recreation directors, nor are we health specialists or dance specialists with undergraduate and graduate degrees in any of these three allied professions. These allied professions are now too highly specialized for us to think there ever can be one professional association that can serve all four fields. What we do understand is *physical* recreation only, some of the health aspects of developmental physical activity, and occasionally some of the social and traditional dances.

In the early 1970s, our late friend and colleague Laura Huelster and I began to deplore the rift that had seemingly inevitably developed in the field since the mid-1960s between the so-called scholars and the so-called practicing professionals. What could possibly be done about this problem? We decided that one approach would be to conjure up a taxonomy that would include both the professional and the scholarly dimensions of our work. With this thought uppermost, we decided upon a balanced approach between the *subdisciplinary* areas of our field and what might be identified as the *subprofessional* or concurrent professional components. By this we mean that what many have called scholarly professional writing (e.g., curriculum investigation, management theory) will be regarded as scholarly endeavor if done well, just as what many have considered to be scholarly, scientific endeavor (e.g., exercise science), if done well, should indeed be regarded as professional writing too (i.e., writing that should ultimately serve the profession).

As part of an effort to close what we regarded as a debilitating, fractionating rift within the field, we developed a taxonomical table to explain the proposed areas of scholarly study and research using *our* nomenclature (sport and physical education terms only) along with the accompanying disciplinary and professional aspects. We agreed upon eight areas of scholarly study and research that are correlated with their respective subdisciplinary and subprofessional aspects in Table 1. Most important, you will note that the names selected for the eight areas do not include terms that are currently part of the names of, or the actual names of, other recognized disciplines and that are therefore usually identified with these other (related) disciplines primarily by our colleagues and the public.

Thus, our position is that we must promote and develop our own discipline of developmental physical activity and our own profession of sport and physical education as described above, while at the same time working cooperatively with the related disciplines and the allied professions (to the extent that interest is shown in our problems). We maintain that by continuing to speak of sociology of sport, physiology of exercise, and so on, the time is ever closer when these other disciplines and professions will really awaken to the importance of what we believe to be *our* professional task (i.e., the gathering and dissemination of knowledge about developmental physical activity through the media of sport, exercise, and related expressive movement, and the promotion of it to the extent that such promulgation is socially desirable).

Table 1

Developmental Physical Activity in Sport, Exercise, and Related Expressive Movement

Areas of scholarly study & research	Subdisciplinary aspects	Subprofessional aspects
I. Background, meaning, & significance	History Philosophy International & comparative study	International relations Professional ethics
II. Functional effects of physical activity	Exercise physiology Anthropometry & body composition	Fitness & health appraisal Exercise therapy
III. Sociocultural & behavioral aspects	Sociology Economics Psychology (individual & social) Anthropology Political science Geography	Application of theory to practice
IV. Motor learning & control	Psychomotor learning Physical growth & development	Application of theory to practice
V. Mechanical & muscular analysis of motor skills	Biomechanics Neuroskeletal musculature	Application of theory to practice
VI. Management theory & practice	Management science Business administration	Application of theory to practice
VII. Program development	Curriculum studies	Application of theory to practice

(General education, professional preparation, intramural sports, and physical recreation, intercollegiate athletics, programs for special populations [e.g., handicapped] including both curriculum and instructional methodology)

VIII. Evaluation & measurement	Theory about the measurement function	Application of theory to practice

I'm certain that you can understand my concern. It is simply this: The end result of a continuation of this splintering of our field of sport and physical education is bound to be a mishmash of isolated findings by well-intentioned, scholarly people not in a position to fully understand the larger goal toward which our profession is striving. Also—and this is vital for us—we will be destined (doomed?)

to perpetual trade status (not *professional* status) as perennial jacks-of-all-trades, masters of none.

Therefore, what I am arguing is that we call ourselves by a name that bespeaks what it is that we study and what we stand for professionally. Laura and I decided to recommend *developmental physical activity* as our term that is similar to such terms as law, medicine, business administration, and so on. The understanding would be that it relates to sport, exercise, and related expressive movement. This term could work at all levels of the education system as well as in public, private, and commercial agencies. It would then be up to us to explain further that this title with three words is an all-encompassing term that refers to the theory of human motor performance in developmental physical activity, theory that is being based increasingly on scholarly and research endeavor of a high order. I honestly believe that this term is understandable and that people (professionals and the general public) would understand and appreciate such linguistic usage. We are the people in the profession that is concerned with physical activity that is used for some sort of worthwhile development throughout a person's life. Any specializations within the profession could develop further by using this name as a point of departure.

The controversy over a name does point up the urgent need for clarity in our use of language, however, not to mention the need to close the "say–do" gap in our professional endeavors. Indirectly it points the way to bridging the ever-widening gap developing among the professional practitioner, the bioscientific researcher, the social science and humanities scholar, and the administrator/ manager and supervisor. I believe most sincerely that increased emphasis on *our own* profession is a truly important point right now, because it is symptomatic of the many divisions that have developed in the past 40 or 50 years in our field. We recognize full well that there are now a number of allied professions represented to a greater or lesser extent in the Alliance. It is not a question of attempting to bring them back into the physical education fold again—they are gone forever. However, in their own interest and ours, we must keep them as closely allied as possible. There are also many related disciplines that are waking up to the fact that developmental physical activity in sport, exercise, and related expressive movement is important to people of all ages. As Jimmy Durante said, "Everybody wants to get into the act!" We should let them all know what we stand for, and then invite them aboard to help us out in various ways.

A Need for Reunification

What is really crucial at the moment, then, is that we seek to bring about a recognizable state of reunification within what we presently call the field of sport and physical education. We do need a new name, but it should be a name that reflects both the disciplinary and the professional aspects of our work. As my figures have shown graphically, prospects for the future will be bleak indeed if the present splintering process is not reversed. We simply must figure out ways and means of unifying the various aspects of our own quasi-profession/quasi-discipline to at least a reasonable degree. Here I am referring to developmental physical activity in sport, exercise, and expressive human movement for those who are qualified and officially recognized and officially certified in the theory and practice of such movement—be they performers, teacher–coaches, teachers of teacher–coaches, scholars and researchers, practitioners in alternative careers, or other professional practitioners in areas not yet envisioned.

Finally—and most frankly—wouldn't we all be sad to see the field to which we have devoted our lives continue to lose ground? We are being outflanked by so many different specialists and specialties that one hardly knows in what area we as a profession still speak with authority. It doesn't have to be this way. If we don't take positive steps to rectify the present development and continuing trend, we will continue to lose professional ground. I believe we deserve a better fate, but we are going to have to plan, organize, and work harder than ever before to earn it!

References

CONANT, J.B. (1963). *The education of American teachers*. New York: McGraw-Hill.

DANIELS, A. (1965). The potential of physical education as an area of research and scholarly effort. *JOHPER,* **36**(1), 32-33, 74.

ESSLINGER, A.A. (1966). Undergraduate versus graduate study. *JOHPER,* **37**(9), 63-64.

HENRY, F.H. (1964). Physical education: An academic discipline. *JOHPER,* **35**(7), 32-33, 69.

HOLMES Group Report, The. Tomorrow's teachers: A Report of the Holmes Group. (1986). East Lansing, MI: Holmes Group, Inc.

VANDERZWAAG, H.J. (1983). Coming out of the maze: Sport management, dance management, and exercise science—Programs with a future. *Quest,* **1**, 66-73.

ZEIGLER, E.F. (1972). A model for optimum professional development in a field called "X". In P.J. Galasso (Ed.), *Proceedings of the First Canadian Symposium on the Philosophy of Sport and Physical Activity* (pp. 16-28). Ottawa, Canada: Sport Canada Directorate.

ZEIGLER, E.F., & McCristal, K.J. (1967). A history of the Big Ten Body-of-Knowledge Project. *Quest,* **IX**, 79-84.

Recent Developments Concerning
the Term Kinesiology

Michael G. Wade
University of Minnesota

Discussions emanating from the 1987 Big Ten director's meeting and two national reports, the Holmes Group Report and the Carnegie Task Force (*A Nation at Risk*), have coincided with a movement nationwide in departments of physical education to redefine their mission, both in terms of the content of their degree programs and in the name of the department and the accompanying degrees. Increasingly the term physical education, most appropriate for programs that license teachers, seems ill suited to describe the current mission of departments of physical education in major universities. The teacher redesign movement will require a discipline degree as a first degree for teacher preparation, and this interfaces nicely with the kinds of 4-year degrees currently being planned and in some places now operational. These activities are not unique to Big Ten institutions, and therefore the 1988 conference was jointly sponsored by both the Big Ten (CIC) and the American Academy of Physical Education.

The December 1988 conference was an "invited only" conference and, with some unfortunate omissions, the institutions represented play key roles in graduate work in our field. By any measure they are considered the leaders. Nationwide, events relative to teacher redesign and the changing role and mission of departments could be seen as driving our need to change and better organize. Academically the field is a diversified set of small scholarly affiliations with a large single professional organization (AAHPERD). While we have a loyalty and historical ties to AAHPERD, it is clear that if we are to press our role in the major university context we must review how much of our time and effort, in the future, will be focused on the preparation of public school teachers and other professionals. This requires reconsideration of both present professional affiliations and the advantages and disadvantages of the term *physical education* as opposed to an alternative name that might better describe our role and mission. If we can reach consensus on a term to describe our field of study and conceptual agreement as to its context, this should provide a basis to develop our influence in several domains, academic, societal, and political.

Since Henry's 1964 paper and the CIC Body of Knowledge conference the same year, the ongoing debate that has never been fully resolved is the issue of whether we are a discipline or a profession. A careful reading of Henry's paper suggests to me that Henry carefully managed to keep both the discipline and professional issues alive by arguing that we are a profession capable of disciplined study within the university context. While this may have satisfied the detractors 25 years ago, my sense is that today the term physical education is one that continues to place us on the defensive in trying to explain and define our mission. Unfortunately, or fortunately, the term physical education is well understood and has historical perspective in terms of its associations with education and teaching in the public domain. Table 1 illustrates and contrasts this point.

The eight points illustrate where we stand both as a discipline and as a profession. Clearly the term physical education for the profession is well established and well understood. From the discipline perspective, what we do is less well understood and less well defined and requires continued justification and explanation. We do not have a single term or a description of our field of study that does for the discipline what the term physical education has done for the profession.

The 1988 conference program comprised a set of papers that focused on what we determined were the central issues facing all of us. The issue of a name

Table 1

**Contrasting Views of the Discipline and Professional Aspects
of Physical Education**

Discipline	Physical education	Profession

Well defined in subdiscipline categories:
  Exercise physiology
  Motor behavior
  Biomechanics
	1. Focus/content	Traditional model now under attack:
		  Carnegie report
		  Holmes report
		  Teacher redesign

Dance as a performing art	2. Performance	Dance education, but activity not well accepted academically
Fragmented, many societies	3. Societal affiliation	Well organized, AAHPERD
?	4. Political influence	Not significant given its size
Policy in place	5. Affirmative action	Policy in place
Poor	6. Minority representation	Variable
Good integration in industry, military, medicine	7. Linkage	Little impact outside public education, sport, and armed forces
No agreement, variety of terms	8. Unified term	Good agreement on the term physical education

was one that permeated the whole conference and was closely aligned to the development of a conceptual statement for our field. Along with this were the companion issues of teacher redesign, certification, the politics and economics of our field, and our position on affirmative action and minority representation. Also, we considered the kinds of contributions and linkages that we should have with the military, industry, and the medical sciences. Finally, we debated the question of where performance (dance and other forms of movement expression) fits as an integral part of a field of study. Physical activity per se has not been well supported generally in academic programs except as a performing art.

The December 1988 conference and the subsequent April 1989 conference find us attempting to reach consensus on a name for the field and a conceptual description of our field of study. This is clearly not a unique situation, but the issues now before us are driven by outside forces and we do not have the luxury of mere idle contemplation! The physical activity triangle (or is it another Trinity!) of performance, discipline, and profession is the current description that appears to enjoy a good measure of support (see Figure 1).

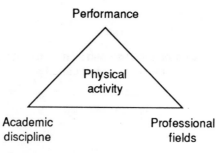

Figure 1 — The physical activity triangle.

There is general agreement that the discipline corner of the triangle might be called kinesiology. Further discussion and negotiation will perhaps allow the term kinesiology to describe all three elements of physical activity. The term itself permits diversity of focus for individual institutions. Thus, while agreeing to a unified term for our field, each institution may vary its program according to its own strengths, mission, and so on. What is important however is that undergraduate and graduate degrees that use the term kinesiology rather than physical education need to reflect some agreement on core preparation. It is not in our collective interest that every single department in the country that now calls itself physical education should feel the wind of change and declare itself overnight to be a department of kinesiology without some fundamental reevaluation of its core preparation and the offerings in its curriculum! At the risk of sounding elitist, it's clear that the term kinesiology for the name of a degree is probably only appropriate in the 50 or 60 universities that have graduate programs focusing on the study and research of physical activity rather than a central mission of preparing teachers and other professionals in the allied health fields.

We have today agreement on a definition for a field of study to be called kinesiology. The Academy needs to develop this definition and take a position on the term to provide further impetus to our task. Agreement on a definition of both the field of study and a core preparation for degree programs that would be granted under the term kinesiology would enhance and bring into focus more precisely the study of physical activity as an academic discipline. Further it would empower the field to better organize itself and perhaps explore the development of some kind of federation that would draw together all of the subdiscipline-based societies (groups that currently abound) and to bring them under one umbrella organization. This would permit those societies to continue to flourish and yet provide a unified voice that would be heard in terms of its views on issues that have implications for the broad area of physical activity, sport, and exercise. I have provided here a brief summary of the activities that began with the jointly sponsored leadership conference in early December 1988, a summary that brings us to this current meeting of the Academy and I think provides an accurate account of the activities, issues, and problems that have been experienced along the way.

Trends in the Changing Titles of Departments of Physical Education in the United States

Jack E. Razor and P. Stanley Brassie
University of Georgia

Change is endemic in higher education, and the academic fields of health, physical education, recreation, and dance are in particular a focal point for disciplinary amelioration and professional redirection. The broad-based fields of health, physical education, recreation, and dance in higher education cannot now be generically described nor easily explained. Changes are occurring that preclude a definition appropriately describing all dimensions encompassing the disciplinary base and professional activities typically associated with the descriptors "health," "physical education," and "recreation," because they are employed in a wide variety of geographically diverse, public and private, large and small, and divergent mission-oriented institutions in higher education. Our professions are sensitive to these changes, as reflected in the reorganization and retitling of academic departments and colleges and in professional commentary (Bird, 1988; Bressan, 1979; Caldwell, 1988; Cicciarella, 1988; Franck, Lockhart, & Nelson, 1986; Greendorfer, 1987; Lucas, 1986; Martens, 1982; Ojeme, 1984; Piper, 1988; Razor, 1988; Sage, 1984; Spirduso, 1988; Thomas, 1987; Vincent, Winningham, & Caldwell, 1988; Word, 1988).

Physical education as an organizational or program descriptor may include a wide variety of functions, such as the basic instruction program designed to accommodate the university student body at large; the undergraduate professional preparation program designed to prepare teachers for all educational levels in the public schools; and undergraduate programs or majors for athletic trainers, coaches, sport administrators, sport journalists, wellness specialists, youth program directors, preschool activity specialists or physical therapists, with the possibility of further specialization within any one of these dimensions. Additionally, there are programs in physical education that are discipline-focused and in which physical education may be studied as a content-based subject matter and not as a field wherein the objective is to prepare someone for vocational pursuit.

At the graduate level not only are there programs designed for continued study and granting degrees in each of the aforementioned programs, but there are also highly specialized degree programs in physical education with a focus on sociology, psychology, social psychology, history, philosophy, biomechanics, physiology, measurement and evaluation, curriculum theory, motor behavior, administration, and newly emerging specializations such as biochemistry of exercise, exercise nutrition, and pharmacology. Further, the term physical education in some sectors of higher education frequently includes the programs and associated activities of intercollegiate athletics, campus recreation, intramural sports, and student activities.

Whereas significant progress has been made in the separation and differentiation of physical education from health education, recreation and leisure studies, dance, and safety education (and there is an increasing number of descriptors employed to identify these fields) in our own profession, considerable confusion still exists with some academicians. In many institutions our colleagues in other sectors of the university tend to view our fields as if they were one, or, if viewed differently, the difference is one of nomenclature as opposed to substance.

Physical education in higher education is no longer a professional field devoted primarily to preparing certified teachers to teach physical education in the public schools. Whereas education is still an important mission, the focus has expanded beyond the schools to include the public, corporate, and government sectors and the myriad of structures and enterprises therein. Additionally, increased attention is now being centered on exercise and sport science. Reflections of these changing foci in physical education in higher education are seen in contemporary curricula and programs, the employment of faculty with increasingly diverse backgrounds in areas other than what has traditionally been called physical education, varied employment opportunities for physical educators, and the changing of titles of the academic units comprising what heretofore comprised physical education.

Accompanying all this, if not being a precursor of these changes in program foci and department titles, has been a significant change in the scholarly dimension of the faculty in physical education in higher education with an increased focus on research, scholarly productivity, and an emerging emphasis on interdisciplinary study. Given the increasing specialization within our disciplines and subdisciplines, the demand for higher standards through accompanying certification and registration by an increasing number and variety of organizations, the inevitable changes occurring in teacher education in both higher education and in the public schools, the evidence of the restructuring of the organizational and administrative format and operation of our academic units in higher education, and the growing independence and diversity of professionals comprising our academic fields in higher education, it is obvious that change has and is occurring and is likely to be the norm for the next decade.

Change occurring in physical education in higher education is increasingly being reflected in the title employed to describe the functions being conducted in the academic department. A wide variety of titles or descriptors and organizational relationships are now being employed by institutions with either the same or different missions. The academic rationale and personal reasons for change are as varied and frequent as the new titles and structures. It is also important to recognize that this phenomenon is occurring in other fields of study and is not unique to physical education nor is it confined to the United States.

A national study was conducted to determine the extent of change occurring in each of the fields of health, physical education, recreation, and dance, the rationale for change, and the ramifications and impact of such change. Specifically the national survey sought to (a) identify the various titles employed to describe the academic units comprising each of the fields of health, physical education, recreation, and dance; (b) determine the status of change in the title being employed to identify each of the academic units; (c) determine the rationale for changing the titles of the units; (d) identify the organizational superstructure accommodating each of the academic programs; (e) determine the impact, if any, that such changes have had on programs in terms of student recruitment, quality of students, faculty expertise, faculty productivity, faculty morale, grant acquisition, budgetary resources, acceptance in the academic community, and university interdisciplinary activity; and (f) relate such variables to the geographic location, size, mission, and type of support of the institution.

As many institutions and departments have changed or may be contemplating change in both title and organizational structure, such information may be of practical importance and the data will be of descriptive value in documenting if and why change is occurring. Further, the information may provide insight as to the future direction of health, physical education, recreation, and dance in their respective roles in higher education. The data obtained may also generate as many questions as they answer. For example, if there are significant changes occurring in physical education in higher education, what will be the ramifications, if any, on physical education as we now know it in the public schools? The possible implications of this question and the subsequent discussions and interpretations are significant for society in general, the public schools, teachers, and state departments of education as well as for those institutions with physical education departments preparing teachers. The question of ramification or consequence also applies contextually to the preparation of other types of professionals now being included in physical education, as well as to programs in which physical education is studied from a disciplinary perspective.

Data collected were from questionnaires sent to 1,327 colleges and universities in the United States as identified in the *HEP 1987 Higher Education Directory*. The investigation was designed to yield information from a broad spectrum of institutions with regard to titles and structures of health, physical education, recreation, and dance. Some institutional respondents indicated that whereas they did not offer degrees in one or more of the fields, there were academic programs, courses, services, and activities in the aforementioned areas and they were appropriately recognized, organized, titled, and staffed by professionals. Of the 1,327 questionnaires sent, 614 were returned for a 46% response rate. The instrument was designed to categorize the respondents in multiple dimensions including institutional type (private/public), size (0-999; 1,000-2,500; 2,501-5,000; 5,001-15,000; over 15,000), mission (significant instruction emphasis, significant instruction emphasis with research, and significant research with instruction), and geographical region (Central, Eastern, Midwest, Northwest, Southern, and Southwest).

Following is a brief summary of the findings that relate to the changes occurring in physical education in higher education. Supporting data in tabular form and descriptive format as well as interpretations and analyses of the changes occurring in physical education (and health, recreation, and dance) are available in a larger, comprehensive technical report, *A National Survey of the Changing Structure and Names of HPERD in Higher Education* (Brassie & Razor, 1989).

Degrees Offered

The data were examined by the type of degrees offered in physical education by institutional type, size, mission, and geographical region. Of the 614 respondents, 76% (467) offered degrees at the bachelor's level, with 42% (199) of these institutions having enrollments of less than 2,500. Of those offering the doctoral degree in physical education, 81% (38) had an enrollment of over 15,000, with 31 of these institutions having a primary mission of research with instruction. Among the responding 51 research/instruction institutions that offer the bachelor's degree, 96% (49) also offer the master's degree and 60% (31) offer the doctorate. With regard to mission, the vast majority of the profession's bachelor's degrees are being generated in institutions in which the primary mission is instruction only—52% (243), and in institutions in which instruction with research is the primary mission—37% (173).

Organizational Structure

The researchers investigated the organizational location of health, physical education, recreation, and dance units and whether they were in the same or different administrative structure. Data were again examined by institutional type, size, mission, and geographical region. Of the 565 respondents to this inquiry, 75% (424) indicated that the areas of health, physical education, recreation, and dance were in the same administrative unit. However, it should be noted that in institutions with enrollments over 15,000, the organizational location of the four areas was almost evenly divided, with 51% (43) being in the same administrative structure and 49% (41) being in one or more different administrative units.

Institutional mission also influences the organizational location of physical education. Of the 306 respondents indicating instruction as their primary mission, 82% (252) were located in the same organizational structure as health, recreation, and dance. Where the primary mission was research with instruction, physical education was located in a different administrative unit, from one or more of the other academic areas, in 43% (29) of the institutions.

Title Changes in the Past 10 Years

Of the 526 respondents in physical education, 23% (119) indicated a change in title had occurred in the past 10 years. Changing the name in physical education occurred far more frequently in institutions with enrollments over 15,000 where 45% (35) reported a title change. Change in the other four enrollment categories ranged from 16% (14) in institutions below 1,000 in enrollment to 24% (18) in the 2,501-5,000 enrollment category. Change was also more likely to occur in research/instruction mission institutions where 38% (25) changed their title, as compared to instruction mission institutions, where only 19% (53) changed their title, and instruction/research mission institutions where 23% (41) changed the department title.

Impact of Title Change on Selected Variables

The study was also designed to determine the impact of the title change on nine selected variables including student recruitment, quality of students, faculty productivity, faculty expertise, faculty morale, grant acquisition, budgetary resources, acceptance in academe, and interdisciplinary activity. For those institutions changing their title in physical education, the most frequent response for six of the nine variables was "no change." However, a significant number of institutions indicated that the title change had a positive impact on student recruitment, quality of students, faculty productivity, faculty morale, grant acquisition, and budgetary resources regardless of the size or mission of the institution.

In the area of faculty expertise, it is noted that the title change in physical education was viewed to have a "dramatic shift" by 19% (22) and "some shift" by 53% (61) of the institutions, for a total of 72% (83) viewing the title change to be related to a shift in faculty expertise. In the area of academic acceptance, 46% (53) viewed the title change to have increased their acceptance in academe, 46% (52) indicated no change, and 8% (9) viewed the title change to have negatively affected acceptance in academe. In the area of interdisciplinary activity, 51% (58) viewed the title change to have increased interdisciplinary activity, 44% (50) thought it had resulted in no change, and 5% (6) thought it decreased such activity. It is also interesting to note that in institutions over 15,000 and with a research/instruction mission, 63% (12) viewed the title change in physical education to have increased grant acquisition. The data for research/instruction institutions of over 15,000 indicate the title change had a positive impact across all variables.

In summary, whereas the most frequent response across all variables was "no change" (with the exceptions of "acceptance in academic community" and "university interdisciplinary activity") for all institutions regardless of size or mission, more institutions viewed the name change to be positive and beneficial than to be harmful. In the areas of acceptance in academic community and university interdisciplinary activity, more institutions reported an increase in acceptance and interdisciplinary activity over "no change." Larger institutions were also perceived to have benefited more with the title change in the area of university interdisciplinary activity than smaller institutions.

Programs Considering a Change in Title

Of the 467 institutions with physical education degree programs, 17% (81) reported that they were considering a change in the title of the department. It appears that a consideration of title change occurred across all institutional enrollment categories. Of the institutions offering degrees in physical education, 6% (5 of 81) in the 0-999 category; 19% (23 of 118) in the 1,000-2,500 category; 14% (9 of 66) in the 2,501-5,000 category; 18% (22 of 123) in the 5,001-15,000 category; and 28% (22 of 79) in the over 15,000 category were considering a change in title. Although institutions with all three categories of institutional mission were considering a title change, it should be noted that 39% (20 of 51) of institutions with a research/instruction mission were considering a title change.

Titles Under Consideration

The 81 institutions considering a title change in physical education identified three title configurations that could be clustered and a fourth category called "other" that included a wide variety of departmental titles—25% (20) identified "sport with a variation" (e.g., sport studies, sport science), 11% (9) identified "human performance with a variation," and 9% (7) identified "kinesiology." The "other" category included a variety of responses making it difficult to draw any conclusions. The category "sport with a variation" appeared most frequently in institutions between 1,000-15,000 enrollment and with an instruction or instruction/research mission. Title change appears to be occurring more frequently in large, research mission institutions when compared to smaller institutions where the primary mission of the college is teaching. These smaller institutions tend to retain a title that includes physical education and perhaps "athletics" or "intramurals." Thus, whereas there appears to be significant change in titles occurring in the profession, the actual number changing may be less than what

Table 1

Titles Being Considered in Departments of Physical Education

Kinesiology	Sport science & movement education
Human performance	Sport science & leisure studies
Sports studies	Sport management
Exercise science	PE & sports programs
Sports science	Human movement studies
HPERD	Human movement
Exercise & sport science	Human performance & sport science
Recreation	Human kinetics & health
Sport, exercise & leisure science	Health & human performance
Sport & exercise science	Human performance & leisure studies
Human performance & health promotion	Human kinetics
Wellness & fitness	Physical culture
Wellness education	Physical education & human movement
Allied health	Exercise & movement sciences
Kinesiology & exercise science	Exercise science
Health & physical education	Exercise science & human movement
PE & exercise science or sport science	Human movement sciences
Recreation & wellness programs	Human movement studies
Exercise & sport studies	Human movement studies & PE
Leisure science	Movement & exercise science
Interdisciplinary health studies	Physical education
Movement studies	Physical education & exercise science
Exercise & movement science (grad. only)	Science of human movement

Note. All respondents are considering one or more of the above titles.

Table 2

Title of Department Currently Assigned
to the Area Traditionally Called Physical Education

Physical education	118
HPER	64
HPE	50

(Remaining titles had fewer than 10 responses)

PE & athletics	PE & recreation
HPER & athletics	Athletics
HPERD	HPED
HPE & leisure studies	HPE & sports medicine
HPER & safety	Health promotion & human performance
Recreation & athletics	Health promotion, PE, & leisure programs
Sport & exercise science	Health education & physical education
Exercise science	HPE & leisure services
Physical fitness & recreation	Health education, counseling psychology
Professional PE	& human performance
Human performance	Human performance & health science
PE, health & wellness	Movement
PE & human development studies	Movement & exercise science
PE & fitness	Movement science & PE
PE & health fitness	Education, PE, & business education
PE & therapeutic recreation	Education & physical education
PE, sport & leisure studies	Education
PE & sport	Sports studies
PER & athletics	Sports & leisure studies
PE & health science	Sports medicine & management
PE & sports	Sports & movement studies
PE & exercise studies	Sports management
PE & intramurals	Exercise science & PE
PE, sport, & fitness administration	Curriculum & instruction
Health education	Teacher education
Health, PE, athletics, & dance	Personal development professions
HPE & athletics	

Note. Descriptors are also inversed and interchanged.

the literature portrays, and informal discussions would indicate when all enrollment categories and the various missions institutions are considered. See Tables 1 and 2 for a list of new titles being considered in departments of physical education and for what the departments are currently named.

Impetus for Considering a Change

Researchers also attempted to determine the reasons for changing or considering a change in the title of the department. The number and type of reasons for changing the title differed across all types of institutions. The 119 institutions that have changed and the 81 institutions considering change in physical education were asked to identify the reasons for their action.

The reasons in order of frequency were 61% (121) "redefinition of focus" of physical education, 39% (77) "increased acceptance in academic community," 36% (71) "success in attracting potential students," 19% (37) "increased possibility for grant acquisition," 16% (32) "legislative mandate," and 10% (19) "relocation into a new academic unit." "Redefinition of focus," "success in attracting potential students," "legislative mandate," and "relocation into a new academic unit" appeared evenly distributed across both institutional enrollment and institutional mission. "Increased acceptance in academic community" also appeared evenly distributed across institutional mission, but was largely concentrated among institutions with enrollments above 5,000. "Possibility for grant acquisition" was largely concentrated in institutions with an enrollment above 5,000 with instruction/research or research/instruction as a primary mission.

It is apparent that two phenomena are occurring with regard to the changing of titles in departments of physical education in higher education: (a) Change is occurring among all type, size, and mission-oriented institutions, with the greater frequency occurring in research-oriented institutions with enrollments over 15,000, and (b) where change does occur, there is more divergence than commonality in the titles selected.

References

BIRD, P.J. (1988). College name change—A rationale. *Journal of Physical Education, Recreation and Dance, 59*(1), 25-27.

BRASSIE, P.S., & Razor, J.E. (1989). *A national survey of the changing structure and names of HPERD in higher education.* Reston, VA: American Alliance for Health, Physical Education, Recreation and Dance.

BRESSAN, E.S. (1979). 2001: The profession is dead—Was it murder or suicide? *Quest, 31*(1), 77-82.

CALDWELL, S.F. (1988). To "energize" physical education—Change dualistic term. *Journal of Physical Education, Recreation and Dance, 59*(1), 11.

CICCIARELLA, C.F. (1988). "Kinesiology" is not the answer. *Journal of Physical Education, Recreation and Dance, 59*(3), 11.

FRANCK, D.M., Lockhart, B., & Nelson, R. (1986, Fall). Should the name by which we are identified—physical education—be changed? *NASPE News, 16,* 4-5.

GREENDORFER, S.L. (1987). Specialization, fragmentation, integration, discipline, profession: What is the real issue? *Quest, 39*(1), 56-64.

HEP higher education directory. (1987). Falls Church, VA: Higher Education Publications.

LUCAS, J.A. (1986). Open forum. *The American Academy of Physical Education News, 6*(3), 8.

MARTENS, F.L. (1982). Why "physical education" should not be "physical education and sport." *Canadian Journal of Health, Physical Education and Recreation, 49,* 12-15.

OJEME, E.O. (1984). Has the name physical education outlived its usefulness? *The Physical Educator, 41*(4), 190-194.

PIPER, R.A. (1988). P.E. recognized as core subject: No name change necessary. *Journal of Physical Education, Recreation and Dance*, **59**(4), 10.

RAZOR, J.E. (1988). The Holmes Group proposal—Implications for physical education. *Quest*, **40**(1), 33-46.

SAGE, G.H. (1984). The quest for identity in college physical education. *Quest*, **36**(1), 115-121.

SPIRDUSO, W.W. (1988). A case for a common name for the academic degree program supporting certification to teach physical education. *Texas Association for Health, Physical Education, Recreation and Dance Journal*, **56**(2), 9-11.

THOMAS, J.R. (1987). Are we already in pieces, or just falling apart? *Quest*, **39**(2), 114-121.

VINCENT, W.J., Winningham, S.N., & Caldwell, S.F. (1988). Department name change: A rationale for kinesiology. *Journal of Physical Education, Recreation and Dance*, **59**(7), 109-110.

WORD, C. (1988). Change perception not name. *Journal of Physical Education, Recreation and Dance*, **59**(5), 15.

Activity, Health, and the Public

Marshall W. Kreuter
Centers for Disease Control, Atlanta

Members of the Academy, international guests, and friends and colleagues of the Alliance: I thank you for the honor and privilege of the invitation to present this lecture, which annually commemorates the distinguished work of R. Tait McKenzie. I want to begin by asking a question, and I direct my question to three groups: (a) the Alliance as a body politic, (b) the leadership of several professions that make up the Alliance, and (c) all of you as individuals. The question is, What is your agenda? Now you may in turn say to me, I have many agendas, which one are you talking about? My response is, your professional agenda . . . what is it you're trying ultimately to accomplish? And, an important related question is, Is your agenda in any way linked to the agenda of the person sitting next to you?

After his inauguration, President Bush named his nominee for Secretary of Health and Human Services: Dr. Louis Sullivan, President of Morehouse Medical School. On this past February 23rd, Dr. Sullivan underwent his Senate confirmation hearings, chaired by Senator Lloyd Bentsen of Texas. After Sullivan's opening statement and an hour or so of questions, Senator John Heinz (R—PA) asked Dr. Sullivan the following question. I will read directly from the recorded transcription:

> SENATOR HEINZ—One last quick question. You had a very commendable opening statement. You identified all the areas of appropriate concern for HHS. But if there is one thing you would like to accomplish . . . that you would like to leave behind as a special legacy . . . what would it be?
> DR. SULLIVAN—Yes, Senator Heinz, there are several . . .
> SENATOR HEINZ—Just one.
> DR. SULLIVAN—Yes, right.
> SENATOR HEINZ—The top one, if there is one.
> DR. SULLIVAN—Yes, right—the top one actually would be greater emphasis and development of health promotion strategies . . . it can lead to major improvements in the health status of all our citizens . . . it is the best investment for improving health and restraining costs for our citizens.

Dr. Sullivan added more about the role of health promotion in "self-empowerment" and "giving individuals more control over their lives" and concluded by saying, "Health promotion strategies would be the number one priority in the Department, because of the many benefits that it would bring to our population. And also it would cause, I think, the biggest bang for the bucks available.''[1] That exchange gives us some sense of the agenda of Dr. Louis Sullivan, the person charged with protecting and promoting our nation's health. We'll return to this issue of agenda later.

My comments this evening are biased by my agenda: public health. That bias is reflected by an emphasis on two things. The first is a focus on the health of populations with an emphasis on prevention. The population focus in public health has grown out of early public health successes in controlling the spread of infectious disease. In the case of an outbreak of disease, the duty of the private physician is to treat the patient, relieve the symptoms, and cure the disease.

Public health workers take a different approach, an approach characterized in this quote by Hippocrates: "The function of protecting and developing health must rank even above that of restoring it when it is repaired." Public health workers begin by sorting through all of the possible explanations for the cause of the disease; when they find the cause, they try to figure out how it is being spread and then try to come up with an intervention that will prevent the disease from occurring.

For example, if they discover that a disease is caused by a bacteria spread via the drinking water, a population-based prevention strategy would involve not only the purification of the water supply, but would also include a comprehensive educational campaign directed at health workers, citizens, and decision makers. Such scenarios have occurred many times over, all around the world, resulting in improved health for hundreds of thousands of people. This is not at all to imply that treatment is frivolous by comparison, but simply that the priority for public health is the health and quality of life of populations through effective prevention—healthy Portland, Maine; healthy Bismark, North Dakota; heart-healthy Harlem; healthy Alabama; healthy America . . . the health of populations.

The second element is perhaps more important than the first: social justice. Our goal is health and quality of life for *all*, not just for those with means. We can celebrate the benefits of health promotion only when we are sure that those with the meagerest of resources are also enjoying its benefits.

It was just about the turn of the century when R. Tait McKenzie left his position at McGill University to become a professor of physical education at the University of Pennsylvania. At that time, the life expectancy in the United States was 50 years; life expectancy in the U.S. today is 75 years . . . think of it, that's 25 years of life per person gained, a 50% improvement! Most observers attribute that spectacular improvement to the rather unspectacular phenomenon I was just talking about: public health. Although the public is enthralled by the wonders of high-tech medicine, star wars surgery, and heart transplants, the lives saved and the suffering prevented by these "media event" procedures is dwarfed compared to those that have resulted from immunizations against infectious diseases (especially for children), water purification, improved nutrition, and environmental controls . . . historic improvements in human health through everyday, unspectacular, "shoe leather public health."

Contemporary public health has had to take its agenda beyond the bounds of infectious disease and environmental control. In addition to making sure that our water is pure (which is no simple task), and that diseases like polio and diphtheria remain virtually nonexistent, public health has turned its prevention energies to today's leading health problems: heart disease, cancer, injuries, suicide, homicide, alcohol and drug abuse, teen pregnancy, preventable problems associated with aging, and of course AIDS.

For these problems, there are no vaccines. Their causes are multiple; they are at once biological and political, environmental and behavioral, individual and collective. We need a better understanding of what causes the unnecessary occurrence of these problems. The word *unnecessary* in this context is used a good deal in the language of public health policy; it's a word worth pondering. Death caused by coronary heart disease at age 45, 50, or 60 is unnecessary; all deaths due to injuries and most lung cancer deaths are unnecessary; AIDS is unnecessary. All of these things can be prevented. I think there is something immoral about identifying a problem and then not doing everything in our power to make available and accessible that which is known to be effective in preventing that problem. In the struggle to address these problems, it has become obvious that it is sometimes insufficient or inappropriate to focus on the prevention of death as our primary outcome; in cases involving older citizens or children with asthma, for example, the key issue isn't death, it is quality of life, the ability to function and perform . . . to be more than alive . . . to live.

Our health promotion and disease prevention work in the last decade at CDC has led us to several important new research and program priorities; one of those priorities I suspect the average citizen wouldn't immediately associate with public health (although R. Tait McKenzie did 75 years ago). It has epidemiological and public health importance of a magnitude far greater than was imagined just a few years ago; it is something that is fundamental to every discipline represented by the Alliance and, therefore, everyone in this room. Without research and program attention to it, I don't think the fields of recreation and leisure studies, or dance, or physical education, or health education would have much meaning. The priority I'm referring to is physical activity.

When public health workers try to link some sort of an event or condition to a health outcome, they refer to that event or condition as an exposure. For example, if cigarette smoking is the exposure, the outcome is an increased risk of lung cancer. We can now be aggressive about making the case that when the exposure in question is an appropriate level and duration of physical activity, the result will be an increased probability of a health benefit. If something is worth doing, it's worth studying and, as St. Augustine might have been suggesting in the following quote, if we're going to study physical activity, we'd best be able to define it: "For so it is, O Lord my God, I measure it, but what is it that I measure?"

Our group at CDC defines physical activity as "bodily movement via skeletal muscles which results in energy expenditure."[2] I like that definition; it's simple, measurable, and to the point. It takes into account a wide range of energy expenditure, from a little to a lot. We now know that you may not need a lot of physical activity to get a benefit, thus every little bit counts! I want to set aside the academic jargon and definitions for a moment to make a point about the way some of us interpret the actions of others. For example, I have this awful tendency to view virtually every encounter I have in terms of its application to the promotion of health! When I read a book, see a play or whatever, I try to translate the lessons learned in terms of my work. So, when I think about different people across cultures and the activities they're engaged in, I conjure up in my mind the potential health benefits they might gain. But, over the years I've learned that the world through my eyes is just that, and it frequently has absolutely no relationship to what others think or what they desire. The truth is, few people who engage in physical activity have health on their minds! I suspect that most people are motivated to engage in physical activity for reasons other than health.

Actually, I don't think that's important . . . what is important is to understand that, as rational beings, something motivates us to act . . . to dance, to hike, to swim, to garden, to walk rather than ride, to propel our own wheelchair rather than be pushed, and so on. And, that "something" is certainly not going to be the same for everyone. So, given our knowledge of the benefits that can accrue from physical activity, if the goal is to attain a health effect, we'd better figure out how to identify and nurture whatever it is that motivates us to action.

I have recently had the pleasure to work with Richard Manoff, a pioneer in the application of marketing strategies to public health. Here is what he had to say about this issue:

> Regrettably, facts do not speak for themselves. Knowledge and truth may empower the mind but they do not necessarily propel it to action. Without sensitive insight into the target audience's perception of a problem and their feelings about the solution, the message, though correct in its science, could prove to be inappropriate. . . . The purpose of the health promotion message is to persuade, not merely to inform, to create a demand within people to take action and not merely to supply them with the truth for their passive intellectual enjoyment.[3]

The physical, emotional, and social benefits of a prudent physical activity routine are now well documented. Physical activity of appropriate intensity and duration reduces the risk of a first heart attack by about one third. We often hear of the so-called major risk factors for coronary heart disease mortality: smoking, hypertension, and elevated serum cholesterol. (Please bear with me because this is an important point.) The term relative risk is used as an estimate of one's chances of experiencing an event given the exposure to a risk factor. A heart attack would be an event, smoking or elevated cholesterol, the exposure. The relative risk for these major risk factors ranges from 2 to 2.7, which means that, compared to someone who is not exposed to smoking, a smoker has twice the chance (a relative risk of 2) of having a heart attack. My colleagues at CDC carried out an analysis in which they were able to show that the relative risk of physical inactivity is of a magnitude comparable to smoking, hypertension, and elevated cholesterol. From the population bias of public health that I mentioned earlier, the impact of physical inactivity on coronary mortality is substantial.[4]

Here is what I mean: Figure 1 shows an estimate of the national prevalence of these major cardiovascular disease risk factors among adults. A very small percentage of the adult population has uncontrolled hypertension, 27% smoke, . . . but nearly 60% are sedentary! Because the relative risks for all of these risk factors are essentially the same, there is absolutely no question that the promotion of physical activity to the population constitutes a major health promotion opportunity.

The benefits of prudent physical activity are by no means limited to heart health.[5] There is good scientific evidence indicating that physical activity improves

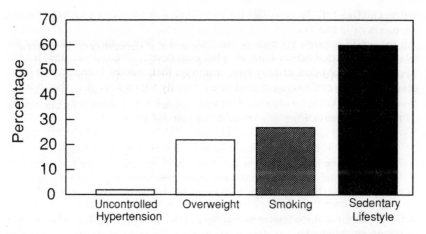

Figure 1 — **National prevalence of CVD-related risk factors (1985 BRFS—22 states).**

the health status of persons with two other important diseases: diabetes (especially Type II or adult onset diabetes) and hypertension. Studies also show that exercise reduces the symptoms of depression, reduces the risk of osteoporosis, and may have a significant interactive effect on smoking and the use of alcohol and drugs. And, research into the relationships between levels of physical activity and central nervous system function, as well as various mental and physical performance variables, is precisely the kind of work that will give us much needed insight into the difficult to measure quality-of-life element I mentioned earlier.

In spite of the benefits of physical activity, it is not without its potential risks, the most obvious being overexertion and injuries (including untimely encounters with automobiles and dogs). Even though the benefits of physical activity far outweigh the risks, prudent judgment is still required. Good judgment is grounded in knowledge; making sure that knowledge is effectively transferred is a primary mission of many of us in this room. I wonder how well we're really doing? Do we have an informed, health-literate society, one that truly understands the benefits of physical activity and is capable of taking appropriate action? With that rhetorical question, I want to spend a few minutes on the life and times of R. Tait McKenzie.

R. Tait McKenzie's achievements were remarkable.[6] In a single lifetime he acquired distinction in three areas, each of which has enriched humanity: physical education, medicine (especially rehabilitative medicine and the practice of physical therapy), and art. He was a renowned sculptor. He created two commemorative medals of special interest to this audience: (a) the medal for the American Academy of Physical Education with its famous "Pass It On" motto inscribed, and (b) the original medal for the American Physical Education Association.

His work in physical education and health began just before the turn of the century when, as a licensed physician, he began teaching at McGill University in Canada with his friend and colleague, James Naismith; he then moved on to accept a faculty position at the University of Pennsylvania. His teaching, research, and philosophy stressed the use of exercise as a means of keeping human beings healthy and well. His writing and work clearly stamp him as an advocate of health promotion.

Historians credit his lectures in hygiene at the University of Pennsylvania as the impetus for that institution's future research and work in public health. I came across a paper he had published in 1913 entitled "The Influence of Exercise on the Heart." It was a delight to read. In spite of the primitive instruments he had to work with, he employed rigorous methods and was strong but careful in his commentary. Here is a quote from that paper:

> If kept within the limits of overstrain and exhaustion, systematic graduated exercise is perhaps the best method of building up the heart size and strength, and even in the most damaged hearts there is no better way of keeping up the tone and efficiency than by movements kept within the limits of fatigue.[7]

He loved athletic competition; the grace, strength, and beauty of human performance inspired his sculpture. He saw participation in athletics as a means of expressing many of the best things humanity had to offer, including the development of self-discipline and the experience of fair play. But ever the educator, McKenzie worked hard to keep athletics as an integral part of the educational program.

McKenzie was a Canadian citizen and, during the First World War, he volunteered in the British Army and was commissioned into the British Royal Army Medical Corps. During the war, he discovered just how physically underdeveloped the population was. He saw the weaknesses exposed by the war as a confirmation of his belief in the health benefits of physical activity, and he campaigned for broad-based physical education to reverse the norm of a sedentary public.

But McKenzie's efforts went unheeded. Historian J.F. Keys attributed the continuation of the nation's sedentariness to our preoccupation with watching rather than doing. He said, "With the new big stadiums came the exploiting of sports as an entertainment industry. The prewar deterioration of the general physique continued under a gleaming exterior of record breaking athletic shows."[8] I wonder what Keys would say today? We've got much, much more to watch, and we don't even have to expend energy to get to the stadium! In fact, we don't even have to get up and walk over to the TV to turn it on, we just use our remote! "Couch potato" says it all, doesn't it?

What was it like in McKenzie's time? In addition to the point I mentioned earlier (that our life expectancy is 25 years greater today) there are, of course, some obvious differences like electronic conveniences and computers, freeways, movies, jet planes, nuclear weapons, and social phenomena like civil rights and women's rights. But there are some other differences in our comparative histories that I found interesting, and I thought you might as well.

When McKenzie began his tenure teaching at the University of Pennsylvania, the population of the United States was one third of what it is today; just under half the population lived in rural areas, and 25% of all jobs were farm related. Today, only 15% of the U.S. population lives in rural areas, and fewer than 2% of the American workforce are classified as farm workers.

In the year that McKenzie graduated his first class at the University of Pennsylvania, there were 30,790 degrees (bachelors, masters, and doctorates) awarded collectively in all of the colleges and universities in the U.S.; of all those degrees, only 19% were awarded to women! In 1985 alone, there were over 600,000 degrees conferred in the United States, and 61% went to women, a mere 300% improvement!

Now I want to ask you women in the audience to be kind in your thoughts and reactions to my next commentary. Like all of us, McKenzie was human; accordingly, he made an occasional faux pax. Even though he was an outspoken proponent of physical activity for men and women alike, he was once quoted as saying that he believed intensive athletic competition by women may lead to the development of knock knees.[9]

I've already mentioned that McKenzie was an advocate of athletic competition; he especially loved the Olympics as an art form and as a means of cultivating human relationships and international diplomacy. He missed only one Olympiad in his lifetime, that due to illness. As for his theory of knock knees he may have been on to something! I have a photo showing Florence Griffith Joyner in the 1988 Olympics on a turn in the 200 meters, and indeed she appears to have knock knees!

The truth is that American men who were Olympic record holders during the midpoint of McKenzie's career would be no match for women today! Olympic record holders in the men's 100, 200, and 400 meters (which included the likes of Frank Jarvis and Archie "The Milwaukee Meteor" Hahn) would be beaten soundly by Evelyn Ashford, Valerie Brisco Hooks, and Florence Griffith Joyner. Even the Olympic record time in the 100 meters set by Harold Abraham, the protagonist of the popular *Chariots of Fire* film about the 1924 games, would have lost to Flo Jo. In fact, I don't think any of the men's Olympic records in the early 1900s would stand up against today's women. And, it's a good thing that Rosa Mota wasn't entered in the marathon in those days. She would have beaten the winner, Michael Theato of France, by 30 minutes and the top American finisher by an hour and a half!

But I'm convinced that McKenzie would have been delighted to learn all of this, primarily because these improvements are a direct reflection of much of the work accomplished by those professionals represented by the Alliance members: better training, better nutrition, better facilities, and more opportunity to engage in an active lifestyle, especially through quality recreation and, of course, progress in equal rights.

Although the demographic and human performance differences between McKenzie's time and our's suggests that we live in quite different worlds, his belief in the fundamental good that physical activity could bring to human beings is as relevant today as it was then. The difference is, we now have the research evidence to support our claims. Remember that it was McKenzie's experience with troops in World War I that led him to believe that the fitness of the U.S. population was generally poor. But, since we have no population-based data on activity status from his time, we can't know for certain just how sedentary the population actually was, especially when you take into account the norms of the time: much higher rates of manual labor, limited modes of transportation, and so on.

But, 75 years later, we do have data that enable us to say with reasonable certainty how active we are . . . here comes that population bias again! Earlier we mentioned that over half of the adult U.S. population was sedentary. Figure 2

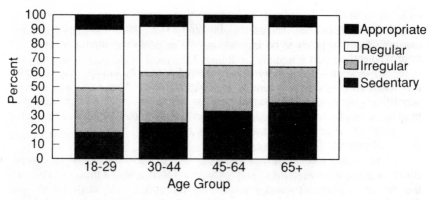

Figure 2 — Prevalence of types of physical activity by age group.

shows us the prevalence of different levels of physical activity by age groups.[10] The bar to the left connotes the 18-to 29-year age group, and the bar to the far right connotes those 65 and older. The blackened part of the bars refers to the portion of each age cohort that reportedly engages in an "appropriate" level of physical activity: one or more activities performed 20 minutes or more per session, three times per week at an intensity of 60% or greater of an individual's cardio-respiratory capacity (this is the standard set for meeting the 1990 objectives). The white portion of the bar refers to "regular" physical activity, which is defined in the same way appropriate activity is defined except that the 60% of cardio-respiratory capacity requirement is not met. The single-hatched portion of the bar refers to "irregular" physical activity, which is defined as one or more activities reported, but the time and intensity is less than 20 minutes per session and less than three times per week. The cross-hatched portion of the bar refers to "sedentary," defined as no activity reported.

The pattern depicted by this figure is disturbing. First, appropriate activity (the level we seek as our standard for health promotion) is alarmingly low, reaching 10% only in the youngest age group. Second, as you follow the bars from left to right, it is clear that as the population ages, the level of regular physical activity (white portion of the bars) decreases, giving way to an increase in sedentariness (cross-hatched portion of the bars).

But after all this hullaballoo about physical activity, is it really a problem? Or is it, to quote Shakespeare, much ado about nothing? Look around you . . . there are joggers and bikers everywhere. Had the terms Reebok, New Balance, and Nike been a part of the Miller's Analogy test when I applied for graduate school in 1961, I wouldn't have had a clue as to what they meant. Sales for athletic apparel has never been higher, physical fitness has become big business, all my friends start the day with a bowl of oat bran and a Jane Fonda or Richard Simmons workout tape, and those of us addicted to golf have to line up to get a starting time as if we were getting tickets to the World Series. Physical activity has become a social norm . . . what's the problem?

The problem has two parts. The first is reflected by some population data we're currently analyzing. Dr. Carl Caspersen on our staff has done a preliminary analysis of the 1984–1987 trends in sedentariness among U.S. adults based on results from the Behavioral Risk Factor Surveillance System. In that 4-year period, sedentariness has increased significantly.[11] No *other* coronary heart disease risk factor appears to be increasing. We're going the wrong way!

The second part is equally troubling. Like most of the beneficial elements in our society, physical activity is only the norm for a segment of our society. Recall that public health bias I mentioned at the outset . . . a focus on populations and a commitment to social justice. What images come to mind when we think of physical fitness? People who appear fit, hard working, graceful, and beautiful, perhaps Florence Griffith Joyner holding the American flag during a victory lap in the 1988 Olympics or fit, active women in a large aerobics class . . . real people. But, consider another image, also of real people. Picture two obese black women having their blood pressure taken. Is there a place for these not-so-fit women in our vision of physical activity? Do the inherent benefits, the "good work" the Alliance stands for, . . . your agenda . . . include these women?

The answer is, "Yes, but!" Actually, these women are two among many who, during the past 2 years, have been involved in a community-based program designed to help minority women (and some men) in a low-income Atlanta neighborhood to reduce their risks of diabetes and hypertension; the mediator is physical activity.[12] Allow me to explode a myth. Here's the myth: Persons who are disadvantaged, however you want to define that (persons without means, of lesser education, the elderly, etc.), are not interested in things like physical activity (dance, aerobics, swimming); they are too busy just trying to survive.

Indeed they are quite busy trying to survive, that's true; the other part is not true. The desire to experience the joys of activity, or any other human experience, is not inherently extinguished because a person is in difficult social, physical, or economic circumstances. The limiting factor is opportunity, not will. The Atlanta program used some of the same principles mentioned earlier in my reference to Richard Manoff, the marketing specialist. Program planners made every effort to understand the agenda of potential participants. When participants were asked what needed to be done to get them involved, here's what they said: make programs available at convenient times, in convenient places; make sure that our access to the place is safe; have child care available; and, make it fun.

And they did all of that. The participation rates were higher by far than anything reported in the literature; participants lost weight and lowered their blood pressure. Here are some faces of physical activity we don't see enough of. I wish R. Tait McKenzie were alive today so that his artistic ability could capture the joy that activity brings to these faces.

A moment ago I used the phrase, "Yes, but!" Yes, there are some wonderfully creative programs like the one in Atlanta (incidentally, many of which use dance as the medium of activity) that do reach those with limited means . . . but they are, in the purest sense, deviations from the norm. I cannot speak for you, but I am embarrassed by that fact. I am ashamed that we are so slow in making progress in reaching all segments of our society. We use the excuse that "they" are hard to reach. "Hard to reach," what a terribly ethnocentric phrase that is; perhaps it would be more accurate and honest to say, "As yet, reaching those with limited means has not become a priority for us." My friends, we have work to do; gaps to close. Although we've made great strides in documenting the substantial health benefits that accrue from prudent physical activity, I'm afraid that in the eyes of decision makers and those who set policy, the value of physical activity is as underappreciated today as it was in McKenzie's time.

I began my remarks this evening with a question: What's your agenda? What's the Alliance's agenda? the Academy's agenda? the agenda of recreation? dance? health education? physical education? The organized, scientifically based promotion of physical activity ought to be a key part of your agenda. We all need to take stock of where we are relative to where we ought to be; we need to take time out of our hectic day-to-day chores to reexamine the philosophic roots of our several complementary professions.

Irrespective of our Alliance affiliation, or whether our primary interests lie in research, instruction, or service, I would urge that as you define your agenda, you look for the common ground. Find a priority issue that is valued by all affiliates so that you maximize the chance for a collective effort. Let me save you a trip to the dictionary and define the word *alliance*: a formal pact or union or confederation between nations in a common cause. Common cause . . . agenda, what is it? Then, once your agenda is delineated, go public. Don't keep it a secret. It is extremely difficult to influence decision makers when neither they nor the constituents they listen to know who you are or what you stand for. Secretary Sullivan's testimony at his confirmation hearings gave you some indication of one of the priorities in his agenda. The extent to which that priority is translated into public policy and support for research and programs is in large part dependent on signals he gets from various groups, especially groups that need to be reckoned with.

What are the characteristics of groups capable of influencing policy, groups to be reckoned with? They are well organized, capable of mobilizing the support of other constituents; they are groups with a clear, discernable, and appealing agenda. Hedrick Smith wrote a bestselling book entitled *The Power Game: How Washington Works*.[13] It is a fascinating and insightful analysis of how things do or don't get done in the highest levels of the Washington bureaucracy. Even though he uses presidential and congressional examples, the process is no less relevant for the environments that you and I work in; after all, schools, colleges, agencies, and professional associations are political environments of one form or another. In his book, Smith repeats two points time and again.

One is the need to set a clear and understandable agenda, making sure that those who need to, know about that agenda. And the second point is the appreciation for just how critical coalitions are in making things happen. Titles or personalities may give you visibility, but power and change come about through action by a strong and committed coalition whose membership shares a common cause. The National Health Objectives for the Year 2000 process now going on here in the United States, the World Health Organization's policy entitled Health For All By the Year 2000, and Secretary Sullivan's position are but a few of the many clear signals that the promotion of health and quality of life is a national and international priority.

The Alliance has every ingredient, including a health promotion gold mine in physical activity, to step forward as a force to be reckoned with in this arena. But, as is the case for an orchestra, to play truly beautiful music, the musicians, however gifted they may be as individuals, must play together from the same arrangement, the same score . . . and they need a conductor, they need leadership.

I began this presentation by asking the agenda question to the leaders of the Academy, the Alliance, and the various disciplines that make up the

Alliance . . . I also asked it of you as individuals. What can we do as individuals to close the gap? I addressed this issue in part at a presentation in 1987 at the Society for Public Health Education (SOPHE) National Meeting in New Orleans. I said then that we need a better understanding of how to implement what we know works! We need more culturally sensitive materials and more facilities for training, and resources for program implementation. I also said that more under-represented minorities are needed throughout our professional ranks. I offered four suggestions for personal action. Actually, they were really just reminders, because you, like me, have heard them all before . . . I suppose the question is, have we been listening?

- Keep this problem on our plate, talk about it in staff meetings, make it an issue.
- Don't set priorities without asking, Are we addressing those at highest risk?
- The leaders in this field should internalize the spirit of affirmative action and act on it, set some personal goals and make a difference.
- And perhaps the most important point, don't even think about doing good for somebody else without first involving them as a part of the entire process in a meaningful way.

Each one of us is a professional with a duty to do good work. Each one of us is an informed citizen of the community we live in. If each of us makes sure that his or her own agenda includes a commitment to closing the gap, doing what we can to make sure that we're not going the wrong way, we will have taken a big step. I want to close by telling you a story that is loosely derived from an essay entitled "The Star Thrower" written by Loren Eisely.[14] I find that the moral fits nicely into the Academy's motto: Pass It On.

A man holidaying in a coastal city somewhere in South America went out for one of his routine sunrise beach walks. As he approached the beach, he saw what appeared to be a dancing figure against the morning sunrise. As he got closer, he saw that his dancer was a young man bending down, picking up starfish, and throwing them out into the surf.

"What are you doing?" he asked the young man. "Throwing starfish into the ocean." "Why?" he asked. "Because the sun will be up soon and if the starfish are left on the beach, the sun will bake and kill them," the young man said. "But there are thousands of miles of beach and millions of starfish," the visitor said. "How can your efforts make a difference?" The young man bent down, picked up a starfish and tossed it far out into the surf and said, "It makes a difference to this one!"

The next day the man looked forward to his morning beach walk and another encounter with the "star thrower." He looked for the young man as he approached the beach but he was nowhere to be found. Disappointed, the man began his walk and, along the way, stopped, picked up a starfish, and tossed it back into the sea, . . . like the Academy's motto, the action had been passed on.

Acknowledgments

I would like to thank Steve Blair, John Burt, Carl Caspersen, Jim Ewers, Stuart Fors, Willie Grissom, and O.N. Hunter for their ideas and suggestions in preparing this presentation. I especially want to acknowledge the assistance of two persons: Andrew Kozar for his thoughtful assistance in obtaining information about R. Tait McKenzie and Sonja Green for her patience and superb skill in preparing the final product and its countless preliminary drafts.

Notes

[1]Dr. Sullivan's comments were taken directly from his testimony given to the Senate Finance Committee chaired by Senator Lloyd Bentsen (D—TX) in SD-215 Dirksen Building, February 23, 1989. Briefing ID: 441224, Federal Information Systems Corporation.

[2]Caspersen, C.J., Powell, K.E., & Christenson, G.M. (1985). Physical activity, exercise, and physical fitness: Definitions and distinctions for health-related research. *Public Health Reports*, **101**, 587-592.

[3]This quote was taken from a paper entitled "Rationale for application of social marketing and use of mass media in prevention" that Richard K. Manoff delivered at the Third National Chronic Disease Prevention and Control Conference, October 19, 1988, Denver, CO. For those interested in a very thorough and readable volume on the topic of social marketing, I strongly recommend Manoff, R.K. (1985). *Social marketing: New imperatives for public health*. New York: Praeger.

[4]The methods used to estimate the relative risk for physical inactivity and cardiovascular heart disease mortality are thoroughly described and discussed in Powell, K.E., Thompson, P.D., Caspersen, C.J., & Kendrick, J.S. (1987). Physical activity and the incidence of coronary heart disease. *Annual Review of Public Health*, **8**, 253-257.

[5]Whereas the strength of the relationship between physical activity and health benefits varies according to the health problem in question and numerous exposure variables, McKenzie would have been delighted to know there is a growing volume of high-caliber science that makes a compelling case for the health promoting effects of physical activity. I recommend one of Dr. Steve Blair's recent publications, which has a very complete bibliography. Blair, S.N. (1988). Exercise, health, and longevity. In D.R. Lamb & R. Murray (Eds.), *Perspectives in exercise science and sports medicine*. Indianapolis: Benchmark Press.

[6]My comments on R. Tait McKenzie do not begin to do justice to his vision of the quality of life and health benefits possible through prudent physical activity. Dr. Andrew Kozar, Professor of Physical Education at the University of Tennessee, Knoxville, was the principal source of my information on McKenzie. He gave generously of his time and expertise by sending me numerous articles, slides, and by providing telephone consultation. For a most interesting overview of the life work of McKenzie, with an emphasis on his art, I recommend Kozar, A.J. (1975). *R. Tait McKenzie, the sculptor of athletes*.

Knoxville: University of Tennessee Press. To get a flavor of McKenzie's philosophy, I suggest McKenzie, R.T. (rev. 1924). *Exercise in education and medicine.* Philadelphia: W.B. Saunders.

[7]McKenzie, R.T. (1913). The influence of exercise on the heart. *American Journal of Medical Sciences*, Vol. CXLV.

[8]Quote by Keys taken from an untitled biographical sketch of McKenzie sent to me by Dr. O.N. Hunter, Dean (retired) College of Health, University of Utah, November, 1988.

[9]Kozar discusses this incident in Kozar, 1975, *R. Tait McKenzie, the sculptor of athletes*, pp. 20-21.

[10]Figure 2 was generated from data in the National Health Interview Survey, Health Promotion and Disease Prevention Questionnaire. These data are presented and described in Caspersen, C.J., Christenson, G.M., & Pollard, R.A. (1986). Status of the 1990 physical fitness and exercise objectives—evidence from NHIS 1985. *Public Health Reports*, **101**, 587-592.

[11]Personal communication with Dr. Carl Caspersen. Analysis of physical activity trends based on prevalence estimates from the Behavioral Risk Factor Surveillance System is in process. Inquiries into work ongoing at the Centers for Disease Control related to the health benefits and trends of physical activity should be directed to Dr. Carl Caspersen, Cardiovascular Health Branch, Division of Chronic Disease Control and Community Intervention, Center for Chronic Disease Prevention and Health Promotion, Centers for Disease Control, Atlanta, GA 30333.

[12]The Atlanta program referenced here is called Community Health Assessment and Promotion Program (CHAPP). CHAPP was initiated through a cooperative agreement between the Centers for Disease Control and the Emory University School of Medicine and is currently funded by the Kaiser Family Foundation. Two unique products are currently available from the project. The *Creative Cookbook: Recipes for Lighter Cooking* is a compilation of recipes developed from weekly food sampling sessions with the CHAPP participants. *Mobilizing a Minority Community to Reduce Risk Factors for Cardiovascular Disease: An Exercise–Nutrition Handbook* is a guide and curriculum that can be used by minority communities in developing, implementing, and evaluating a community-based exercise nutrition program. Both products can be obtained from Dr. Robert Curry, Department of Community Health, Emory University School of Medicine, 69 Butler Street SE, Atlanta, GA 30303. Phone (404) 589-3612.

[13]Smith, H. (1988). *The Power Game, How Washington Works.* New York: Random House. This book provides more than a description of how America's political system works, it offers detailed insight into the subtle and not-so-subtle forces that make things happen in any modern-day bureaucratic system. Part III, entitled Big Games of Power, offers some ground rules that need to be reviewed by anyone who finds themselves in a political arena, regardless of the setting.

[14]Eisely's "Star Thrower" essay appears in a collection of essays by the same name. The reference is Eisley, L. (1978). *The Star Thrower.* New York: Harcourt Brace Jovanovich.

Resolution

Whereas the number and diversity of descriptors of academic programs and administrative units related to the study of human movement is now in excess of 100, and;

Whereas the basic conceptual framework of this body of knowledge differs from university campus to campus, and;

Whereas a multitude of degree titles, program names, and administrative rubrics has produced confusion regarding the nature of the study of movement, even among academicians who work in the field, and;

Whereas unanimity in description and a nationally accepted definition of the body of knowledge would provide a stronger sense of purpose, higher visibility in the academic community, and a greater understanding of the discipline by the public;

Therefore, be it resolved that the Academy recommends that the subject matter core content for undergraduate baccalaureate degrees related to the study of movement be called kinesiology, and that baccalaureate degrees in the academic discipline be titled kinesiology.

The Academy encourages administrative units, such as departments or divisions, in which the academic study of kinesiology is predominant, to adopt the name kinesiology. Finally, in any situation in which an administrative unit feels comfortable in describing the totality of its components by the title of the body of knowledge, the Academy recommends that this descriptor be kinesiology.

Comment

The purpose of the resolution is to give description to an academic discipline. The resolution is not intended to legislate changes in professional preparation programs and/or degrees. Kinesiology is the study of human motion. Among key concepts in this body of knowledge are (1) energy, work, and efficiency, (2) coordination, control, and skill, (3) growth, development, and form, (4) culture, values, and achievement.

Motion to adopt the resolution was passed at the business meeting of the American Academy of Physical Education on April 19, 1989.

PRESIDENTS

American Academy of Physical Education

*1926-30	Clark W. Hetherington	*1966-67	Arthur A. Esslinger
*1930-38	Robert Tait McKenzie	1967-68	Margaret G. Fox
*1938-39	Robert Tait McKenzie	*1968-69	Laura J. Heulster
	Mabel Lee	1969-70	H. Harrison Clarke
*1939-41	John Brown, Jr.	1970-71	Ruth M. Wilson
*1941-43	Mabel Lee	1971-72	Ben W. Miller
*1943-45	Arthur H. Steinhaus	1972-73	Raymond A. Weiss
*1945-47	Jay B. Nash	1973-74	Ann E. Jewett
*1947-49	Charles H. McCloy	1974-75	King J. McCristal
*1949-50	Frederick W. Cozens	*1975-76	Leona Holbrook
*1950-51	Rosalind Cassidy	1976-77	Marvin H. Eyler
1951-52	Seward C. Staley	1977-78	Louis E. Alley
*1952-53	David K. Brace	1978-79	Marguerite A. Clifton
*1953-54	Neils P. Neilson	1979-80	Harold M. Barrow
*1954-55	Elmer D. Mitchell	1980-81	Aileene S. Lockhart
1955-56	Anna S. Espenschade	1981-82	Earle F. Zeigler
*1956-57	Harry A. Scott	1982-83	Edward J. Shea
*1957-58	Charles C. Cowell	1983-84	Henry J. Montoye
*1958-59	Delbert Oberteuffer	1984-85	David H. Clarke
*1959-60	Helen Manley	1985-86	G. Alan Stull
1960-61	Thomas E. McDonough, Sr.	1986-87	Margaret J. Safrit
1961-62	M. Gladys Scott	1987-88	Robert M. Malina
1962-63	Fred V. Hein	1988-89	Waneen W. Spirduso
1963-64	Carl L. Nordly		(current)
*1964-65	Eleanor Metheny	1988-89	Charles B. Corbin (elect)
1965-66	Leonard A. Larson		

---

*Deceased

The Academy Papers

With comprehensive coverage of current topics and contributions from the foremost scholars in the field, The Academy Papers are an invaluable resource for every physical education professional and student.

Physical Activity and Aging, Volume 22
Waneen W. Spirduso, PhD, and Helen M. Eckert, PhD, Editors
These 17 papers explore the major issues associated with the contributions of health, fitness, and motor skills to successful aging.
1989 • Paper • 208 pp • Item BSPI0220 • ISBN 0-87322-220-2

Physical Activity in Early and Modern Populations, Volume 21
Robert M. Malina, PhD, and Helen M. Eckert, PhD, Editors
The 10 papers in this volume detail the evolution of physical activity in society including: early man, modern man's ability to adapt to sedentary occupations, diseases of the advanced society, the health of children, and the health of aging.
1988 • Cloth • 120 pp • Item BMAL0180 • ISBN 0-87322-180-X

The Cutting Edge of Physical Education Research, Volume 20
Margaret J. Safrit, PhD, and Helen M. Eckert, PhD, Editors
The contributors in this fascinating volume explore the state of the art and the future of research in exercise science, sport and exercise psychology, motor learning, pedagogy, sport history, philosophy of sport, and biomechanics.
1987 • Paper • 136 pp • Item BSAF0098 • ISBN 0-87322-098-6

Effects of Physical Activity on Children, Volume 19
G. Alan Stull, EdD, and Helen M. Eckert, PhD, Editors
This authoritative volume provides an up-to-date examination of the impact of exercise on the physical, moral, emotional, and intellectual development of children.
1986 • Paper • 174 pp • Item BSTU0049 • ISBN 0-87322-049-8

Limits of Human Performance, Volume 18
David H. Clarke, PhD, and Helen M. Eckert, PhD, Editors
These intriguing papers explore how age, psychological influences, morphological and physiological characteristics, heat, biomechanics, and other factors can limit performance.
1985 • Paper • 144 pp • Item BCLA0099 • ISBN 0-931250-99-4

Exercise and Health, Volume 17
Helen M. Eckert, PhD, and Henry J. Montoye, PhD, Editors
Leading scholars provide an extensive analysis of the relationship between exercise and heart disease, osteoporosis, amenorrhea, obesity, aging, arthritis, mental health, and other factors.
1984 • Paper • 160 pp • Item BECK0056 • ISBN 0-931250-56-0

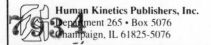 **Human Kinetics Publishers, Inc.**
Department 265 • Box 5076
Champaign, IL 61825-5076

Call TOLL FREE for Credit Card Orders
1-800-DIAL-HKP (1-800-342-5457)
1-800-334-3665 (*in Illinois*)
FAX (217) 351-2674
(VISA, AMEX, MC)